BUILDING QUERIES

Using Microsoft Access 2010

F. Mark Schiavone, Ph.D.

Sycamore Technical Press
www.sycamoretechnicalpress.com

Preface

Microsoft Access is a powerful database management system. It provides easy to work with tools that assist you in the management of your database.

One of the most common actions you can take against a database is to ask questions or *query* the data. This ability to ask a specific question and obtain useful results is at the core of why databases are so useful. Formally, the question is constructed as a *select query* - one of several types of queries we'll explore in this book. Select queries can be very simple or contain *criteria expressions* and/or *parameters* in order to focus or narrow your results. Against a database of every street address in the United States, one can imagine asking the question *who lives at the address 123 Maple Avenue as it appears in any town in the country?* Another possible question of this database might appear as *how many "123 Maple Avenue" addresses are there in the United States?* In both cases these questions would formally be constructed as a select query before being submitted against the database data.

Select queries are powerful and easily the most common query type you will work with. We'll explore them in some detail in order to understand how criteria expression assist in narrowing your questions so that the desired results are achieved. We'll also explore how to create select queries that pull data from multiple tables, and summarize data by grouping, counting, and/summing numeric or currency data. Additional topics will explore how to manipulate fields and join properties, as well as creating functions to convert or modify field data in the results.

In addition to select queries, we'll also explore the two other classes of queries: action queries and SQL-specific queries. Action queries are typically used to maintain the data in a database. They can delete, update, or append data in a table as well as make new tables from existing data. When you add criteria expressions to an action query you further refine the action in a manner similar to using criteria expressions in select queries. The last group of queries, SQL-specific, give you the ability to join data from two or more tables, create or modify tables directly through a query, or pass a query from Microsoft Access to an ODBC (Open Data Base Connectivity) database server such as Microsoft SQL Server or MySQL Server.

Manual Conventions

Throughout this manual reference is made to various components of the software. Tabs, ribbons, groups, command buttons, and windows and views appear in boldface type, for example, **OK** and **Font**. Keystrokes appear in boldface italic type, for example, ***Ctrl + V*** and ***Enter***. When possible, the words *select* and *choose* have been used in this manual to allow you the option of using either the mouse or keyboard. Throughout this manual you'll find the following helpful items:

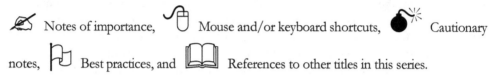 Notes of importance, Mouse and/or keyboard shortcuts, Cautionary notes, Best practices, and References to other titles in this series.

Table of Contents

Introduction

This short course is designed to provide the reader with the skills necessary to create a variety of queries using Microsoft Access. The reader will learn how to create both simple and complex select queries that ask specific questions concerning data stored within a database. Queries that summarize, group, and total information will also be covered, as well as queries that serve as the underlying data source for complex pivot tables. Action queries , which perform specific maintenance and data manipulation tasks, are also covered in detail.

Queries in Microsoft Access are powerful tools and serve a variety of purposes – including acting as the data sources for other complex objects such as forms and reports. Generally, any query created in Microsoft Access adheres to the ANSI SQL (American National Standards Institute – Structured Query Language) or ISO SQL (International Standards Organization – Structured Query Language) standards and thus, learning queries in Microsoft Access may also serve as a useful platform to learn other variants of the SQL language. In those instances where the SQL language in Microsoft Access differs significantly from the SQL standard, those instances will be noted.

This course was originally designed to be delivered in the context of workplace training. When working with staff in a busy corporate or governmental organization I found it important to streamline the approach and design courseware that did not serve as a systematic review of every button you could push in an application. Rather, the approach then, as now, has been to identify and focus on the most important tasks required to get a specific job done. It is my sincere wish that upon completion of this material you'll find that such a task-based focus will leave you with the skills required to create and maintain useful queries for your database.

Chapter 1 | Overview of Queries

A *query* is a database object that can perform any of the following tasks:

- Provide records that satisfy a particular question asked of the database data.

- Perform housekeeping tasks, such as delete or copy records, append data, create tables, or merge values from two fields.

- Create summary views of the data by providing totals, cross tabulations, or pivot tables.

In all cases, a query reduces to a stored command that is run each time the query is opened. Queries in Access are written in *SQL* (Structured Query Language - the letters are pronounced individually), which is a common query language used among major database systems.

Access uses a graphical interface, the **Query Design View**, so you can generate most query types without using SQL directly. Note, however, that each query may be viewed, edited, or written entirely using SQL rather than the **Query Design View**. For some query types (those that pass commands to other, non-Access databases), you must construct the query using SQL.

Types of Queries

There are three broad categories of queries in Access:

- *Select queries* ask specific questions of the data. Select queries may work with one or more tables from the database. You can limit the fields that the query uses to display the results and/or uses to formulate the specific question. Questions are constructed using criteria and/or expressions.

- *Action queries* conduct some action against a table. These queries are generally considered to be maintenance or administrative functions and are frequently used to create new tables, delete or update existing records, or append records to an existing table.

- *SQL-specific* queries permit Access to interact with larger database systems. These queries may not be created using the graphical **Query Design View** features. The query is constructed by typing a SQL statement and, when run, it is typically passed to another database. A SQL-specific query may be either a select or an action query, although some database systems may limit the degree to which a SQL-specific query may modify its database objects.

Each of these query categories contains specific types that are discussed in the following tables.

Types of Select Queries

Name	Description
Select	This is the simplest and most commonly used query. It retrieves data from one or more tables and presents it in a datasheet. You can (in most cases) edit this data and update the original records. Select queries may use *criteria* or *expressions* to return specific records.
Parameters	A select query which uses a *parameter* that you supply at the time the query is run. The parameter value is used as an expression to filter the results. You can enter the parameter in a dialog box, or the query can get the value from an existing form.
Totals	Calculates sums, counts, averages, or use other types of summary functions.
Crosstab	Summarizes (sums, counts, or averages) data in one field (usually a *primary key*) and arranges the summary data in a matrix, grouped against two or more related fields. An example might be a summary of the count of all employee educational degrees (left column), arranged by department (top row).

Types of Action Queries

Name	Description
Append	Adds data from one or more tables to another group of one or more tables.
Delete	Removes records from one or more tables. Delete queries always delete entire records.
Make Table	Creates a new table consisting of data from one or more tables.
Update	Makes changes to data in one or more fields.

Types of SQL-Specific Queries

Name	Description
Union	Combines the results of two or more select queries into a single result set.
Pass-Through	Sends commands directly to an ODBC-compliant database. ODBC (Open Database Connectivity) is an industry standard for inter-database communication via SQL.
Data Definition	Used to create tables or modify tables in Access via SQL commands.

Select Queries and Editing Data

Most select queries will return results using a **Datasheet**, which is presented in the **Datasheet View**. With few exceptions, the data you view may be edited in the **Datasheet View**. Editing the displayed data will immediately update the data in the underlying table. This behavior is different from other common desktop database systems and is not generally seen in server-based databases.

The situations in which you may not edit data from a select query include the following:

- The results are from a *summary* or *crosstab* query. These query types do not display editable data.

- The field is a result of a calculation due to an expression. Other fields may be edited provided they are displaying data directly from an underlying table and not as a result of an expression.

- There are three or more tables referenced in the query, and the relationship joins between the three tables effectively models a many-to-many join (joins from the left-most to the right-most table are one-to-many and many-to-one). Some fields may be edited, depending on the number of primary key fields involved as well as other factors.

- The results are generated from a SQL pass-through query. These queries are read-only.

- There is no referential integrity established between the tables or queries which serve as the query's record source.

- The query's **Recordset Type** property is set to *Snapshot*.

 When you encounter a select query that may not be edited, any of the following may apply: typing does not change the displayed data; a message is displayed once you have edited data informing you that the changes cannot be saved; or you receive a error message that the record is locked.

Queries and Your Database

It is rare to find a Microsoft Access database that does not include queries as part of the suite of objects. A database developer might define queries for several reasons, including:

- Producing commonly-requested views of a subset of a larger pool or data. This subset may be derived from one or more tables.

- Serving to provide a subset of data to another database object such as a form or a report. Although forms and reports may use tables as their direct data source, it's quite common to see queries being used instead. By creating a query that narrows or filters a form or a report's data, you have an easy to manage object that can be modified as needed in order to keep the utility of the form or report current to your needs.

- Performing maintenance tasks on some scheduled frequency. You can create a pair of queries, one append and one delete, that can be configured to archive data from one table (perhaps based on a date/time field) with the effect of moving old data from a production to an archive table.

Another common mode you'll discover is the creation of *ad hoc* queries. These are created to answer a quick question or to conduct some specific maintenance task (such as handling the renaming of a department within an organization). This type of query is created once and then discarded or deleted. The intent is to keep the list of queries down to the most useful or frequently used, yet still create queries to answer a quick question or perform a unique maintenance task.

SQL Statements

The major focus in this book is creating queries using the **Query Design View**, which is a powerful and easy to use graphical editor for query construction. When a query is created using this tool there is always an underlying version of the query converted into SQL text. SQL, or Structured Query Language, is a standard language for submitting queries to nearly any database. Where appropriate, some chapters will end with a brief discussion of how the queries in that section would appear as SQL statements. For the casual user of Microsoft Access these sections should be considered optional. However, if you intend to use queries as data sources for forms, reports, or controls on those objects you should find these SQL sections to be helpful in future work.

Chapter 2 | Creating Queries

Regardless of the type of query you wish to create, all queries begin with the same general procedure. In Access you have two options when you create a query: work directly using **Query Design** tool or use the **Query Wizard** to provide assistance. We will begin creating queries using the **Query Design** tool. Following that we will briefly review the types of queries you can create using the **Query Wizard**. This Wizard is useful for working with certain types of specialty queries, however, any of the queries it creates can also be created using the **Query Design** tool.

The reason we will bypass using the **Query Wizard** to create a simple query is that this wizard isn't of any particular use - it simply adds fields from one or more tables to your query. The wizard completely omits the creation of any criteria which focus or narrow the results returned by your query. By stepping directly into **Query Design View** you are becoming familiar with the very graphical interface that makes query creation so useful using Microsoft Access.

Using the Query Design View

Query Design View is used to graphically generate select and action queries from scratch. Working in this view you can add or remove tables and queries from the **Table Area**, add fields to the **Field Grid**, establish criteria expressions, and view query results. This view also provides the tools to change between query types.

When working with queries, three views are available:

- **Query Design View** provides the graphical tools to create and modify queries.

- **Datasheet View** shows the query results. If the query is an action query, this view shows the records that will be acted on and is separate from actually running the query. Information on action queries appears in Chapter 10.

- **SQL View** is a simple text window that displays the SQL statement that defines the query. When working with SQL-specific queries, this is also the view used to create the query (Query Design View is not available to SQL-specific queries).

In addition, two views are also available which are not directly related to queries (they are also available to tables and forms) yet provide sophisticated data analysis tools:

- **PivotTable View** for creating interactive summary views of complex data. Pivot tables are similar to crosstab queries but are far more powerful.

- **PivotChart View** creates charts from Pivot Table data.

Creating a Query Using Query Design View

The process for working in **Query Design** view is straightforward. You first select one or more tables or queries which will either feed data for your query, or will be the target of an action query. You then work graphically to create your query. The design environment gives you full control over the type of query, the tables and their fields which will become part of the query, the join types you use (if working with multiple, related tables), and the criteria expressions needed to work on a subset of the underlying data.

Queries can be the data source for other queries. Both Microsoft Access and the SQL standard permit such nesting. In Access, most wizards and tools used to select data for a query will allow you to choose among tables and other queries as a data source.

How to Create a Query in Design View

In this example we will add two tables: staff and staff skills, from the *Projects and Staff* database. The design for this database is discussed in Appendix A and is available for download from the www.sycamoretechnicalpress.com website.

Step 1.   From the **Create** ribbon, in the **Query** group, choose **Query Design**. The **Show Table** dialog box will appear as illustrated below:

Step 2.   Select the desired table or query as your data source and select **Add**. If you require two or more tables or queries, continue this process until all objects

have been added to your query design. When you are done select **Close**. The **Query Design View** will appear similar to the following:

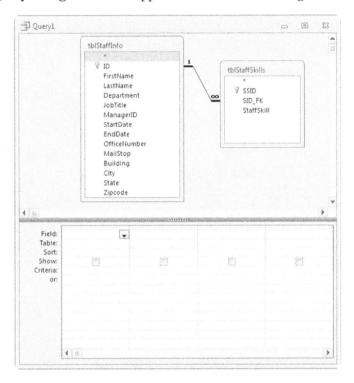

There are two parts to the **Query Design View**: the upper pane (the **Table Area)** shows the tables and/or queries that will supply the fields used to create the query. In the illustration above, two related tables have been chosen in Step 2. These tables are related in a *one-to-many* join that models the fact that each staff may have zero or more skills associated in the tblStaffSkills table. Both tables list their associated fields. Both tables also begin that list with an asterisk (*) which serves as an *all fields* selector. Dropping the asterisk into the lower portion of the window will automatically add all fields from that table to the query.

The lower pane contains the **Criteria Grid**. This area is where you denote which field or fields will be part of the query, as well as what special criteria (search expressions), sort orders, visibility, grouping, and other special attributes will be applied.

Step 3.   Add one or more fields to the **Criteria Grid**. You may either double-click on the desired field or click and drag it onto the grid area. In the illustration below, the fields *LastName* and *FirstName* from the *tblStaffInfo* table, and the *StaffSkill* field from the *tblStaffSkills* table have been added to the grid:

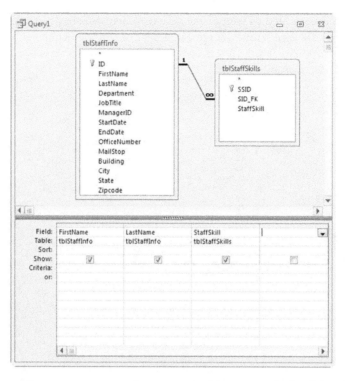

Step 4.   Depending upon your needs, you may wish to consult the following section for more details concerning how to further modify your query:

Add or remove a table or query from your design – Page 9

Add or remove fields – Page 11

Run the query – Page 13

Modify join types between tables or queries – Page 62

Create *Criteria Expressions* to filter query results – Page 20

Create a totals query to summarize numeric – Page 53

Create a *Crosstab* or *PivotTable* query to summarize complex information – Page 79

Or create an *Action query* to update, append, or delete data or to create a new table – Page 100

Step 5. After you have modified your query using the options above, if you wish to save the final design either choose **Save** from the **Quick Access** toolbar, or close the query. If you close an unnamed or unsaved query Access will prompt you:

If you select **Yes** name the query. Choosing **No** closes the query design without saving it. **Cancel** returns you to the **Query Design View** without saving the query.

Managing the Query's Record Source

The tables and/or queries displayed in the **Table Area** of the **Query Design View** constitute the *record source* for the query. They supply the data that the query will act against, either to display the results of a select query or to modify the data as the result of running an action query.

Tables and/or queries are selected as record sources when you initially create the query and interact with the **Show Table** dialog box. At any time, you can add or remove tables or queries from the **Table Area**.

How to Add a Record Source

The query must be opened in **Query Design View** to add additional tables or queries.

Step 1. From the **Query Tools | Design** ribbon, in the **Query** Setup group, select **Show Table**. The **Show Table** dialog box similar to the following will appear:

Step 2. Select the **Tables** or **Queries** tab to view only tables or queries, respectively, or select the **Both** tab to view all potential record sources.

Step 3. Select the desired table or query from the list of objects, and then choose **Add**.

Step 4. Repeat Steps 2 and 3 as desired to add additional tables or queries.

Step 5. Choose **Close**. The newly-added tables and/or queries will appear in the **Table Area** or your query.

How to Remove a Record Source

The query must be open in **Query Design View** to remove a record source.

Step 1. In the **Table Area**, select the table or query to remove by clicking once on its representation.

Step 2. Press *Delete*.

 You can also right-click on the desired table and choose **Remove Table**.

Any fields associated with the removed table or query will be removed from the **Field Grid**.

 You cannot undo the removal of a table or query. Any criteria or expressions deleted from the removed fields are lost.

Managing Fields

When you construct a select or an action query, you add one or more fields from a table or query in the **Table Area** to the **Field Grid**. Fields placed in this region of the **Query Design View** serve to display results and/or specify criteria or expressions.

For each field displayed on the **Field Grid**, you can add criteria, control field visibility, set sort orders, and control summary functions. Establishing criteria in fields is discussed starting on page 21. Working with summary options is introduced on page 53.

How to Add All Table Fields to a Query

You must be in **Query Design View** to work with fields.

Step 1.   In the **Table Area,** locate the **All Fields (*)** indicator from the desired table or query object.

Step 2.   Drag the **All Fields** indicator from the table or query object onto the **Field Grid**, or double-click on the **All Fields** indicator.

How to Add Individual Fields to a Query

Step 1.   In the **Table Area,** locate the desired field from the table or query object.

Step 2.   Drag the field from the table or query object onto the **Field Grid**, or, double-click on the field.

 Double-clicking on a field places it as the next available field displayed in the **Field Grid**. Dragging a field gives you control over the final location. When you drag and release a field between existing fields, Access inserts the field between the existing ones.

When working with related tables or queries, add fields from the *one* side of the join to the **Field Grid** first, then add fields from the *many* side of the join later. The data that will repeat between records will appear on the left-hand side of the datasheet.

How to Remove Fields from a Query

Step 1. Position the mouse pointer over the **Field Grid**, immediately above the field name.

Step 2. When the mouse pointer changes to a dark arrow, click on the field.

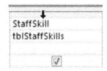

Step 3. Press *Delete*.

 You cannot undo the deletion of a field from a query. Any criteria or expressions associated with the field will be lost.

How to Move a Field

By moving a field in the **Field Grid**, you change the order in which the field is displayed in the **Datasheet View**.

Step 1. Position the mouse pointer over the **Field Grid**, immediately above the displayed field name.

Step 2. When the mouse pointer changes to a dark arrow, click on the field and release the mouse button.

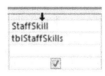

Step 3.   Reposition the mouse pointer above the field name. When the mouse pointer changes to a selection arrow (as shown in the following illustration), click and drag the field to the desired location.

Step 4.   Release the mouse button.

 You can also move several adjacent fields at once. In Step 2, hold down the mouse button and drag the selection area to include all the desired fields. Release the mouse and continue with Step 3, dragging from any of the selected fields.

Viewing Query Results

Once you have added the desired fields, and perhaps criteria to narrow your results, the query is ready to run. In Access, running select and SQL-specific queries simply involves changing to **Datasheet View**. When you run an action query, there is a special **Run** command that will commit the action query.

Points on Viewing Query Results

- A select query that displays all of a table's fields and does not contain any criteria will yield a datasheet that is functionally the same as viewing the table in **Table Datasheet View**.

- The majority of select queries will display data in **Datasheet View**; this data can be edited. Take care not to inadvertently change field values when working in this view. See page 3 for a discussion of conditions that limit the editing of data. Refer to the section beginning on Page 14 for details concerning use of the *Recordset Type* property to prevent edits to your query's display of data.

- All the standard sorting, finding, and filtering operations available to tables in **Datasheet View** are also available to query results.

- When you view the results of an *action query* using **Datasheet View**, you are viewing the records that will be acted upon by the query. The query is not actually run until you use the **Run** command. You will always be warned about the impact of an action query after using the **Run** command. Once you agree to run the query, there is no undo command available. Action queries are discussed in Chapter 10.

How to Change Query Views

Use this procedure to move between any query view. Depending upon whether you are working on your query in **Query Design** view or are viewing the results of your query, the view options are located to the far right of either the **Query Tools | Design** or the **Home** ribbon, respectively.

Step 1.   On the **Query Design** or the **Home** ribbon, select the drop-down list associated with the **View** button.

Step 2.   From the list of views available, select the desired view. Use the following table as a guide.

View	Description
DataSheet View	Displays the query results in a datasheet.
PivotTable View	Opens the PivotTable designer. If a PivotTable has been previously created, that view is opened.
PivotChart View	Opens the PivotChart designer. If a PivotChart has been previously created, that view is opened.
SQL View	Shows the query's underlying Structured Query Language expression. All Access queries are expressed in SQL.
Design View	Opens the query design window.

Query Properties

Queries have properties that are saved with the query. Most of these properties detail how the query will return data. For most query purposes, properties do not require adjustment.

How to Change a Query Property

You must be in **Query Design** or **SQL View** to adjust query properties.

Step 1.   If you are in **Query Design View**, select the query by clicking anywhere in the **Table Area**, but not directly on any of the table representations. This step is not required if you are in **SQL View**.

Step 2.   From the **Query Design** toolbar select the **Properties** button, or from the
            Show/Hide group choose **Property Sheet**. A **Property Sheet** similar to the
            following will appear:

Step 3.   Select the text box for the desired property.

Step 4.   Type a new property value, or select a new property from the drop-down list, or
            choose the *ellipsis (...)* to evoke the **Builder** and use it to create a new property
            value.

     Not all properties have a builder or a drop-down list.

     Pressing *F1* while in a property text box will open on-line help for that
            property.

Common Select Query Properties

Property	Description
Description	Specifies a descriptive phrase for the query.
Default View	Determines whether the query view will default to datasheet, pivot table or pivot chart.
Output All Fields	Controls whether all fields from all tables and/or queries in the Table Area are displayed. When the default value No is applied, only those fields in the Field Grid will appear in the results.
Top Values	Specifies whether all records, or only the *top n* (example: top 100) or *top percentage* (example: top 25%) of records are returned. You need to apply sorting to at least one field in order for this property to return sensible results.
Unique Values	Controls whether the query will only return records where every displayed field value is unique across all records. Only available for select, append, and make table queries. The default value is No. Cannot be set to Yes when Unique Records is set to Yes.
Unique Records	Controls whether the query will only return records where every field value (including those not included on the Field Grid) are unique. Only available for select, append, and make table queries and then only for queries involving two or more joined tables or queries. The default value is No. Cannot be set to Yes when Unique Values is set to Yes.
Record Locks	Specifies the type of record lock applied to the records making up the query results. The choices are Edited Record (default), All Records, or No Locks. Locking prevents other users from making simultaneous changes to the underlying record source. Locks are only applied when you are actually editing data in Datasheet View.
Recordset Type	Controls whether the query's results may be edited (*Dynaset*) or not (*Snapshot*). The default is *Dynaset*. An additional option, *Dynaset (Inconsistent Updates)*, is not recommended as it temporarily overrides some referential integrity settings.
Order by	Specifies a sort order that has been applied to the query results in Datasheet View. This property is generally set when a user sorts a query result and saves the query design.
Max Records	Controls the maximum number of records returned by the query. When blank (default), there is no limit applied.

Field Properties

Each field in a query has a set of associated properties. These are generally used to control how the data are presented. Field properties are only available from **Query Design View**. They are not available in **SQL View**.

How to Change a Field Property

You must be in **Query Design** to adjust query properties.

Step 1.   From the **Field Grid**, select the desired field.

Step 2.   From the **Query Design** toolbar, select the **Properties** button, or, from the **View** menu, choose **Properties**. A **Property Sheet** similar to the following will appear:

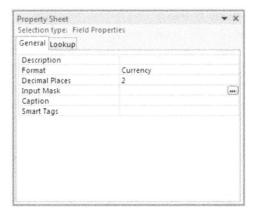

Step 3.   Select the text box for the desired property.

Step 4.   Type a new property value, or select a new property from the drop-down list, or select the *ellipsis (...)* to evoke the **Builder** and use it to create a new property value.

Not all properties have a builder or a drop-down list. Pressing *F1* while in a property text box will open on-line help for that property.

Common Field Properties

Property	Description
Description	Sets a descriptive text string for the field.
Format	Controls the formatting applied to the field data. Available only for certain data types such as *Number* or *Currency*.
Decimal Places	Sets the number of significant digits. Available only for certain data types such as *Number* or *Currency*.
Input Mask	Controls how data is entered into the field.
Caption	Specifies the contents of the **Status Bar** when the field gains the focus.
Smart Tags	Associates certain types of data (for example, dates) with other Microsoft applications or web-based data sources.

 When a field has a format or an input mask applied at the table level, those values are inherited by the query but are not displayed as field properties. The field properties in a query are used to override any table-level properties.

Printing Query Results

When you view query results in **Datasheet View**, the results can be printed or viewed in **Print Preview**. Although this is a quick and easy method to obtain printed results, it is not the preferred method. Reports offer complete control over formatting, grouping, and sorting of data and are therefore the preferred method of obtaining printed information from the database.

How to Print Query Results

You must be in **Datasheet View** for the **Print Preview** command to be available.

Step 1.   Select the **File** tab, then choose **Print**.

Step 2.   Choose among the following options.

Option	Description
Quick Print	Sends the query data sheet to the default printer without any further prompts.
Print	Opens the **Print** dialog box where you can select a printer, set printer properties, control the number of copies or set the print range.
Preview	Displays the query data sheet in print preview mode. From there you may set parameters concerning page and margin sizes and page orientation, or choose to export the data set to another format such as Microsoft Excel.

SQL Select Statements

When you create a query using the **Query Design View** it is actually implemented as a SQL (Structured Query Language) statement. You can see the text-version of any query you create by changing from **Query Design** or **DataSheet View** to **SQL View**.

Some actions discussed in this chapter, such as changing the format property of a particular field do not map to specific SQL statements. However, the majority of the design actions you make while in **Query Design View** do convey to specific SQL statements.

The syntax for a select query is straightforward and takes the form below. Note that reserved SQL works appear in bold text and optional clauses are enclosed in square brackets. SQL statements are always terminated using a semi-colon (;).

SELECT *Fieldlist* **FROM** *Tablename* [**ORDER BY** *direction*];

The following table cites some simple examples of Select queries.

SQL Statement	Description
SELECT LastName, FirstName FROM tblStaffInfo;	Returns the first and last names from all records in a table named tblStaffInfo.
SELECT * FROM tblStaffInfo;	Returns all fields from the tblStaffInfo table. Note that the asterisk (*) means *all fields* when located in the *FieldList* area of a SQL statement.
SELECT * FROM tblStaffInfo ORDER BY LastName ASC;	As the previous example except the records are ordered by LastName in alphabetical order.

Chapter 3 | Criteria Expressions

Criteria (also known as a *criteria expression*) are conditional statements that are evaluated as either being *True* or *False* on a record-by-record basis. When the statement evaluates to *True*, that record is displayed in the query results if running a select query, or used as the basis of action if running an action query. Queries become powerful database tools when you apply *criteria expressions* to one or more fields.

Criteria have the effect of limiting the records a query returns or acts upon. Criteria can be framed as statements containing a question such as *"Who lives in Bethesda, Maryland?"* or *"Which employees have budgeting skills?"* or *"Who works in the Human Resources department AND has project management skills AND was assigned to the new employee manual project?"*

Criteria expressions in Access are not case sensitive. In a criteria expression, the text *Management*, *management*, and *MaNaGeMeNt* will all return the same results.

Points on Criteria Expressions

- Criteria must be constructed such that for each field value evaluated, the result of the evaluation is either True or False.

- Criteria must be syntactically correct. Access will alert you immediately when you create syntactically incorrect criteria and attempt to move to another cell in the Field Grid or change to Datasheet View.

- Some criteria require *delimiters* such as quotes around text and the pound sign (#) around dates. When the wildcard operator, (*) is applied the criteria should begin with the reserved word LIKE. In cases where you may have omitted these items and Access can deduce the correct syntax it will make adjustments to your criteria. When Access is unable to understand your criteria statement as typed it will generate an error message and you'll need to manually correct any syntax issues.

- Criteria may be applied to any query type as a method of reducing or restricting the returned records. When used in an action query, they restrict the records that will be acted upon.

- Placement of criteria in specific cells in the Field Grid has bearing on how the criteria are interpreted. Pay attention to the row and column you are working in when constructing a criteria expression. The spatial relationships between individual criteria and the Field Grid are discussed in following sections.

The Field Grid and Criteria Expressions

You will achieve different logical expressions depending on where you enter criteria expressions in the **Field Grid.** Use these rules when creating criteria expressions:

- Each field is represented as a column in the **Field Grid**. To create a criteria against a specific field, the expression must be entered in the column corresponding to that field.

- There are two different types of criteria rows in the **Field Grid**: *Criteria* and *Or* rows. All criteria expressions must be entered in either a *Criteria* or an *Or* row. The remaining points discuss the spatial relationship between these rows.

- Expressions entered in the *Criteria* or in the *Or* row for any field column act only against the values in that field.

- Expressions entered in several fields but all on the same *Criteria* or *Or* row act together, banded by the logical AND operator.

- Stacking expressions in the same field column but in the *Criteria* and in the *Or* rows relates the expressions together using the OR operator.

- Combining a mixture of expressions in various field columns and *Criteria* or *Or* rows creates more complex logical statements. The criteria in any given row are addressed as a logical unit and are evaluated first. Criteria between rows are connected using the OR operator and are evaluated after criteria in any given row are evaluated.

- Text and date data types must be *delimited* while numeric, currency, and Yes/No values do not require delimiters. Text values are delimited using double quotes (") and date values are delimited using the pound (#) sign. Thus, the values "Washington" and #July 4, 1776# are correctly delimited. As previously mentioned, Access will attempt to add delimiters when missing from your expression.

The following illustrations outline this behavior. For simplicity, only the effect for select queries will be discussed, although the principle for focusing an action query by using criteria is the same.

Placing a single expression in a single **Criteria** cell as illustrated above will return all records where the *State* value is equal to *DC*.

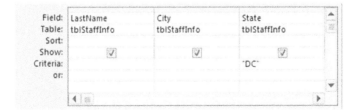

Placing expressions in *two* criteria cells *on the same row* results in the display of all records where the *City* field is equal to *Bethesda AND* the *State* field is equal to *MD*.

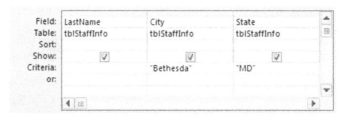

As illustrated below, placing criteria in the same column but in the **Criteria** and the **Or** row results in a query that will return records where the *State* value is equal to *DC OR* the *State* value is equal to *VA*.

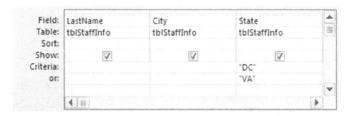

Placing two criteria in the same **Criteria** row but only one criteria in the **Or** row results in a query that returns records where the *LastName* is equal to *King AND* the *State* is equal to *DC OR* all records where the *State* is equal to *VA*.

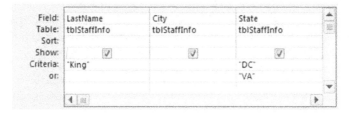

Lastly, creating a matrix where there are multiple criteria on both the **Criteria** row and the **Or** row results in a query that returns records where the *LastName* is equal to *King* AND the *State* is equal to *DC* OR the *LastName* is equal to *King* AND the *State* is equal to *VA*.

How to Create a Criteria Expression (Generalized Procedure)

Step 1. Select the cell where the desired field column and criteria row intersect.

Step 2. Type the criteria expression. Types of criteria expressions and specific examples are addressed in the next section.

Step 3. To create a multiple-criteria query, repeat Steps 1 and 2. Use the discussion beginning on page 21 as a guide to the spatial relationships between cells in the **Field Grid** and their corresponding meaning as expressions.

Step 4. Run the query by switching to **Datasheet View**.

Step 5. If desired, save the design of your query.

Types of Criteria

You can generate a variety of criteria expressions to suit your specific needs. The overall categories of criteria include:

- Literal expressions, which specify the exact field value to be used as a criteria.

- Wildcard expressions, which permit you to apply a broader range of potential values that will satisfy your criteria.

- Operator expressions, which specify ranges under which values may satisfy your criteria.

- Parameters, which permit you to enter one or more of the criteria terms immediately before the query is run. Depending on how it is constructed, a parameter may be a subset of any of the above-listed criteria types.

- Functions, which return some result that is then included as part of the overall criteria. Functions and formula expressions are discussed in Chapter 5.

Literal Expressions

When you enter text, numeric, or date values into a **Criteria** cell, only records that exactly match your typed value will be displayed, or if running an action query, will be acted upon. Literal expressions begin with an *Equals sign* (=).

Literal Expressions

Field Type	Comments
Text	Type the value as plain text. When you leave the criteria cell the value will automatically be enclosed in double quotes. **Example:** ="Human resources"
Numeric	Enter the value as a regular number (omit currency symbols and thousands separators). **Example:** =74000 *or* =345.004
Date/Time	Enclose the date or time value in pound signs (#). Generally you can use any unambiguous date format. **Example:** =#01/01/2013# *or* =#January 01, 2013#. Note that these two examples would retrieve the same records. Note also that Access will not enclose dates within the pound sign automatically.

The use of the pound sign (#) as a date delimiter is unique to Microsoft Access. The SQL standard (as applied by all major database applications) treats dates as text literals.

Operators

Operators are mainly mathematical symbols used for comparison and to specify ranges. The less than (<) and greater than (>) operators may work on numeric or text fields.

When an operator is used in a text field, it evaluates the expression based on the ordinal position of letters in the alphabet. The expression >*Mary* would return records that are alphabetically *beyond* the value *Mary* when alphabetically sorted.

Common Expression Operators

Operator	Name/Purpose	Example
=	Equals operator	= "Bolivia"
<	Less than	< 500
<=	Less than or equals	<= 500
>	Greater than	>500
>=	Greater than or equals	>=500
<>	Not equal to	<>"Bolivia"
Null	Null (used for comparison)	<> Null *(reads "is not null")*
Is Null	Is Null (finds Null values)	Is Null
Is Not Null	Is Not Null (finds non-null values)	Is Not Null
=""	Is Empty (finds *Empty* values)	="" (note there is no space between the double quotes)
Between	Between (for specifying numeric or date ranges)	Between #01/01/1999# AND #01/01/2003#
In()	In (uses a list for comparison)	In("Smith", "Jones", "Baker")

Examples of Operator Expressions

Example	Description
>400	Finds all values greater than 400.
>0 AND <=100	Finds values greater than zero and less than or equal to 100.
<=50 OR >=100	Finds values less than or equal to 50 *or* greater than or equal to 100.
>#01-Jan-2000#	Finds dates from 02 January 2000 and later.
Between #01/01/1999# AND #12/31/2000#	Finds dates that fall in the range between 01 January 1999 and 31 December 2000.
>L	Finds all field values that begin with the letter *M* and beyond (M-Z).
<=C	Finds are field values that begin with the letter A, B, or C.
<>"Brazil"	Finds all values other than Brazil.
Is Not Null	Finds all values that are not null.
Is Null	Finds all null field values.
=""	Finds all empty field values.
Between #Jan 01, 80# AND #Dec 31, 89#	Finds all dates in the 1980s.
In("MD", "VA", "DC")	Finds all field values equal to either MD, VA, or DC.

When working with the greater than (>) or less than (<) operator, you cannot include wildcards as part of the expression.

The difference between **Null** and "" (empty) is that **Null** is interpreted as meaning *I don't know if a value exists* and empty is interpreted as *I know that there is no value*. Whether a field can accept **Null** and/or empty values is controlled by setting field properties when a table is designed.

Wildcards

You can use wildcards to provide a broader range of functionality to your criteria expressions. Wildcards broaden the conditions under which a criteria is resolved to *True*. For example, setting a criteria to the literal expression *="Smith"* in a Last Name field will only return records with that exact last name. Setting a wildcard expression such as *Like "Smith*"* in the same field will return field values such as *Smith, Smithfield, Smithson,* etc.

Common Expression Wildcards

Wildcard	Description	Examples
*	Matches any number of characters. May be placed at the beginning , the end, or enclosing a text string.	wa* finds *Wabash, Washington.* *ton finds *Washington, Reston.* *on* finds *Oneida, Monmouth,* and *Reston*
?	Matches any single alphabetic character.	T?P finds *TAP, TIP,* and *TOP.*
[ ]	Matches any single character within the brackets.	T[AI]P finds *TAP* and *TIP* but not *TOP.*
!	Matches any single character *not* in the brackets.	T[!AI]P finds *TOP* but not *TAP* or *TIP.*
-	Matches any one of a range of characters. The range must be specified in ascending (A-Z) order.	T[I-Z]P finds *TIP* and *TOP.*
#	Matches any single numeric character. Only used in numeric fields.	5#5 finds *505, 515, 525,* etc.

When you enter an expression containing a wildcard, the **Like** operator is automatically added to the beginning of your expression.

With the exception of the # symbol, wildcards are intended to be used in text fields only. If the international settings for your computer accept text in date values, you can use the * and ? wildcards when searching for month names: **Example**: "*aug*" will find all dates in August.

If you need to search for a character reserved as a wildcard, enclose it in square brackets. **Example:** [?] will search for the question mark. To search for paired square brackets, enclose them in square brackets. **Example:** [[ ]] will search for empty square brackets.

Examples of Operator and Wildcard Expressions

Example	Description
Like "Fin*"	Finds *Finance* and *Financial.*
="T?P"	Returns all three-letter field values that begin with T, end with P. The middle character does not matter. Example: TIP, TAP, TOP.
Like "[a-d]*"	Finds values where the first character is either A, B, C, or D.
="T[a-i]P"	T[AI]P finds *TAP* and *TIP* but not *TOP.*
= "T[!AI]P"	T[!AI]P finds *TOP* but not *TAP* or *TIP.*
=200#	Finds all numeric values that begin with *200.*

Parameters

A parameter causes a query to first prompt you for one or more criteria. After you type the requested information, the query uses the information for the criteria. This technique permits queries to use a more flexible approach to criteria expressions. Any query can become a parameter query by including a word or phrase enclosed in square brackets, [ ], into a criteria expression.

Points on Parameters

- Parameters are created by including paired square brackets, [ ], in an expression.

- The text enclosed by the square brackets will appear as a prompt in an input box when the query runs. You enter a criteria value into the input box, and the query is run using that value in place of the parameter.

- Adding additional parameters to one or more criteria creates a multiple parameter query. Access will display a separate input box for each parameter.

- In a query based on multiple parameters, you can control the order in which the parameter dialog boxes appear.

- Parameters may be incorporated into expressions containing wildcards. This permits the expression to be resolved under broader conditions than when using literal expressions.

- Parameters may be incorporated into formula expressions. The expression is not resolved until you enter the parameter value.

How to Create a Parameter Query

Step 1.   Open an existing query or create a new query.

Step 2.   Select the desired **Criteria** cell.

Step 3.   Enter the parameter expression. Use the following table as a guide.

Option	Example	Description
Literal expression	[Enter the state]	The value typed into the input box must exactly match field values.
Wildcard	Like "*"&[Enter Department]&"*"	Because wildcards are added to the beginning and end of the expression, text typed in the input box may show up anywhere in a field value.
Range Between Two Dates	Between [Enter a start date] AND [Enter an end date]	You will be prompted twice. Dates need not be enclosed in pound signs (#) when using parameters.
Upper or Lower Limit	>=[Enter a lower limit for invoices]	Whatever number is entered will serve as the expression to return numeric values equal to or greater than the entered value.

Step 4.   To create additional parameters, repeat Steps 2 and 3.

Step 5.   Run the query by switching to **Datasheet View**. For each parameter you created, a dialog box similar to the following will appear:

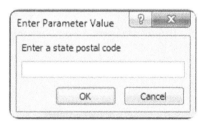

Step 6.   Type a value for your parameter into the input box, then choose **OK,** or, use the **Cancel** button to abort the query.

Step 7.   If desired, save your query.

The *ampersand* (&) used in the previous examples is the *concatenation operator*. Its purpose is to combine string literal values. For example, the expression 8+4 resolves to 12 whereas the expression 8&4 resolves to 84.

Controlling the Order of Parameter Query Prompts

If you have two or more parameter statements in the criteria cells of a query, Access steps through each cell and displays a separate dialog box corresponding to each parameter. The default order is the order of the fields, from left to right.

To control the order in which the parameters appear, you first enter your parameter statements in the particular criteria cells, then use the **Query Parameters** dialog box to specify the desired order of display.

How to Control the Order of Parameter Query Prompts

Step 1.   Open an existing parameter query (with two or more parameters) in **Query Design View**, or create a new query containing two or more parameters.

Step 2.   From the **Show/Hide** group on the **Query Tools | Design** ribbon, choose **Parameters**. A dialog box similar to the following will appear:

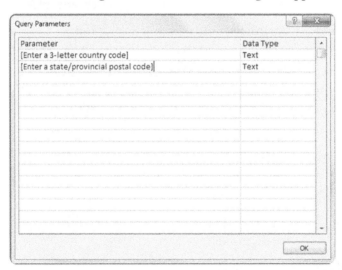

Step 3.   In the Parameter column, enter each of your criteria as they appear in the criteria cells. Parameters will appear in the order listed in the window.

Step 4.   Choose **OK**.

Step 5.   If desired, save the design of your query.

If you only include a subset of your parameters in the Query Parameter window, the remainder will appear in the same order that they appear in the Query Design grid.

The second column in the Query Parameters window allows you to specify a data type for the parameter dialog box. The default value is the Text data type. If a parameter statement is in a field other than the text data type, you can specify the correct data type in the Query Parameter window.

If you create a parameter query and set properties in the **Query Parameters** dialog, and then choose to remove the parameter in the criteria grid, you must also remove the parameter in the **Query Parameters** dialog box – otherwise users are still prompted for parameters that no longer apply as criteria.

SQL Criteria Statements

SQL handles criteria expressions following the **WHERE** clause. Simple criteria map to equivalently simple SQL statements. Statements that AND and/or OR clauses together may get a bit more complicated as Access includes parentheses around clauses to specify the order in which each clause is processed. For example, AND clauses take precedence over OR clauses, and like multiplication, division, addition and subtraction in Algebra, individual clauses (or operators) are enclosed in parenthesis to clearly control how the SQL statement is to be interpreted. Remember that 8+(2/4) yields 8.5 while (8+2)/5 equals 2. The parenthesis specify the order in which a particular operation takes place.

Although you can implement a parameter query in SQL using Microsoft Access, this feature is not a component of the SQL standard - it is exclusive to Access.

To implement a criteria expression in SQL you add the **WHERE** clause plus one or more criteria (the square brackets denote optional clauses):

SELECT *Fieldlist* **FROM** *Tablename* [**WHERE** *Wherecondition*] [**ORDER BY** *direction*];

The following table cites some examples of Select queries with criteria.

SQL Statement	Description
SELECT * FROM tblStaffInfo WHERE Department="IT";	Returns all fields for employees associated with the IT department.
SELECT * FROM tblStaffInfo WHERE Department="IT" ORDER BY StartDate DESC;	As the previous example except records are ordered with the most recent hires listed first and the first-hired staff listed last.
SELECT tblStaffInfo.FirstName, tblStaffInfo.LastName, tblStaffInfo.City, tblStaffInfo.State FROM tblStaffInfo WHERE (((tblStaffInfo.State)="DC"));	Returns FirstName, LastName, City, and State fields from the tblStaffInfo table where staff state is *DC*.
SELECT * FROM tblStaffInfo WHERE (((tblStaffInfo.City)="Bethesda") AND ((tblStaffInfo.State)="MD"));	Returns staff records (all fields) where the staff city equals *Bethesda* and the staff state is *MD*.
SELECT * FROM tblStaffInfo WHERE (((tblStaffInfo.State)="DC")) OR (((tblStaffInfo.State)="VA"));	As above except state is *either* DC *or* VA.
SELECT * FROM tblStaffInfo WHERE (((tblStaffInfo.LastName)="King") AND ((tblStaffInfo.State)="DC")) OR (((tblStaffInfo.State)="VA"));	Returns records where staff last name is *King* AND staff state is *DC* OR any staff record where staff state is *VA*.
SELECT tblStaffInfo.FirstName, tblStaffInfo.LastName, tblStaffInfo.City, tblStaffInfo.State FROM tblStaffInfo WHERE (((tblStaffInfo.LastName)="King") AND ((tblStaffInfo.State)="DC")) OR (((tblStaffInfo.LastName)="King") AND ((tblStaffInfo.State)="VA"));	As above but returns only those records for staff with the last name of *King* who live either in *DC* or *VA*.
SELECT * FROM tblStaffInfo WHERE (((tblStaffInfo.City) Like "*on*"));	Returns all fields from tblStaffInfo where *on* appears *anywhere* in the city field (example, *Oneida*, *Monmouth*, and *Reston*).

Chapter 4 | Manipulating Fields

When you a run a select query Access orders the fields according to their left-to-right placement within the criteria grid. Likewise, the rows of data are presented according to any indices (including primary keys) established in the underlying tables. If no such index exists the results are presented in the *natural order*, which generally is the order in which data were originally entered into the table or tables.

By manipulating fields in **Query Design View** you can change the ordering of columns or rows of data, control visibility of fields, and even combine two or more fields into a single hybrid field. These design modifications are saved in the query specification and continue to be asserted each time the query is run.

Sorting Query Fields

You can sort a query either in **Query Design View** or from **Datasheet View**. When sorting in **Datasheet View** you use the same tools available to sort table data.

Points on Sorting Query Fields

- You can sort on one or more fields. When sorting multiple fields, Access sorts the fields from left to right. The fields need not be adjacent to one another, but you may need to move fields to achieve the desired sorting. Refer to page 12 for instructions on moving fields.

- When you apply a sort order in **Query Design View**, the sort becomes part of the SQL statement for the query.

- Sorting while in **Datasheet View** (and saving the query design) stores the sort order in the query's *Order By* property.

- Sorting applied in **Datasheet View** and stored in the query's *Order By* property takes precedence over sorts applied to individual fields in **Query Design View** (e.g., sorts that become part of the SQL statement).

- The *Order By* property-specified sort may be removed in **Datasheet View** by selecting the **Toggle Filter** button in the **Sort & Filter** group.

- Sorts stored in the query's SQL statement must be removed by modifying the **Sort** cell for specific fields while in **Query Design View**.

How to Apply a Sort in Query Design View

This approach stores any sort specifications as part of the query's SQL statement. You should be in **Query Design View** for your sort specification to become part of the query's SQL statement.

Step 1.   For the field you wish to sort select the **Sort** cell.

Step 2.   Choose the desired sort option from the drop-down list.

Option	Description
Ascending	Sorts alphabetically for text, increasing number order for any number fields, or from oldest to most recent (or future) values for date/time fields.
Descending	Sorts reverse alphabetically for text, decreasing number order for any number fields, or from most recent (or future) to oldest values for date/time fields.
(not sorted)	Field is not sorted. Any ordering applied to the table will take precedent.

Step 3.   Save the query design if desired.

How to Apply a Sort in Datasheet View

This approach stores the sort order in the query property **Order By** provided the query design is saved after the sort has been applied. It overrides any sort applied using **Query Design View**, although it can quickly be removed by selecting the **Filter** button from the **Datasheet View** toolbar.

Step 1.   Open the query in **Datasheet View**.

Step 2.   Select the field or fields to sort.

Step 3.   In the **Sort & Filter** group of the **Home** ribbon, select the **Sort Ascending** button to sort in ascending order, or, select the **Sort Descending** button to sort in descending (reverse) order. Alternatively you can choose a sort order from the drop down box associated with the field header.

Step 4.   Save the design of the query to save the sort order.

 To remove a sort order applied in **Datasheet View**, open the query in **Datasheet View** and deselect the **Filter** button on the **Datasheet View** toolbar. Alternatively, open the query in **Design View** and open the **Properties Sheet** dialog box. Remove any text in the *Order By* property.

Field Visibility

Fields can be hidden in one of two ways. From **Query Design View** you can specify that a field is not visible. While viewing results in **Datasheet View**, you can hide or unhide fields as well. Hiding or unhiding fields using one view does not affect the settings of the other view, although field visibilities modified in either view are saved with the query. Any hidden field that contains *criteria* still participates in the filtering of query data.

If you modified field visibility in **Query Design View** you must use that view to reset or change those settings. If you were working in **Datasheet View** when you modified field visibility, you must return to that view to make changes.

How to Control Field Visibility in Query Design View

Step 1.   To hide a field, remove the check from the **Show** cell for the desired field, or, to show a hidden field, place a check in the **Show** cell for the desired field.

Step 2.   Save the query design if desired.

How to Hide Fields in Datasheet View

Step 1.   Select the field or fields you wish to hide. Note that they must be adjacent when selecting two or more fields.

Step 2.   **Right click** on the column header – do not click on the column header drop down arrow.

Step 3.   From the short cut menu, choose **Hide Fields**.

How to Unhide Fields in Datasheet View

This procedure only unhides columns hidden when in **Datasheet View**.

Step 1.   **Right click** on any column header.

Step 2.   From the short cut menu, choose **Unhide Fields**. A dialog box similar to the following will appear:

Step 3.   Place a checkmark in any field you wish to unhide.

Step 4.   Choose **Close**.

Step 5. • Save the query design if desired.

Renaming Fields

There may be situations where it is desirable to rename a field in a query. You may have similarly named fields in two or more tables and wish to reduce confusion, or the field name may not make sense to someone running the query. You would also rename fields if you combine two or more fields, or use an expression as the source of data for a new field. In the latter two examples, if you do not rename the field, Access will name the fields *Expr1*, *Expr2*, etc.

Fields are renamed by entering an expression in the **Field** row. You specify a new field name, a colon, and the existing field name. For example, entering the term *Last Name:LastName* will cause the column heading to appear as *Last Name* rather than the field name of *LastName*.

How to Rename a Field

You must be in **Query Design View** to rename a field.

Step 1. Select the cell containing the desired field name.

Step 2. Position the insertion point to the beginning of the field name.

Step 3. Type a new field name, then type a colon (:) to separate the new name from the existing field name.

 Renaming fields in a query is one way to solve problems with difficult to understand field names in a table (perhaps the table was created by another person or is linked to a database server). When you rename fields in a query and then use that query as the data source for any form or report, those objects inherit the renamed fields.

Combining Fields

You can combine the values of two or more fields into a single field in a query as long as the involved fields are all of the same data type (if they are of different data types, you can use a type conversion function in the expression). A common use of this feature is to combine first, middle, and last name fields in a query so the results read as an individual's full name.

You enter an expression to combine two or more fields in the **Field** row. You specify a new field name, a colon, and an expression to combine two or more existing fields. The ***ampersand*** (&) is used to combine field names. Example: Full Name: [FirstName] & " " & [MiddleName] & " " & [LastName]

This syntax has the following points:

▪ The text to the left of the colon will appear as the column header once the query has been run.

- A colon is used to separate the new field name from the expression.

- If field names contain embedded white space, you must enclose the field name in square brackets, [ ]. Note that Access will enclose all field names in square brackets once you created your expression.

- If the query is based on two or more tables and a field name is common to both tables, you must indicate which table the field comes from. Use the syntax [table name].[field name]. The period is used to separate a table name from a field name.

- The ampersand, &, is used to combine the fields. If you need to add numeric field values together, use the plus sign instead. Note that the plus sign behaves like the ampersand with text fields.

- If you need to separate field values with a space or add an additional character, such as a comma, include the spaces or other characters enclosed in quotes.

For example, the expression:

Mailing Address:[Address] & ", " & [City] & ", " & [State] & " " & [Zip]

Will produce a column in the results table named **Mailing Address**. A sample result might appear as:

1600 Pennsylvania Avenue, Washington DC 20500

If the expression had been entered as: MailingAddress:[Address]&[City]&[State]&[Zip] it would have instead produced an output similar to the following:

1600Pennsylvania AvenueWashingtonDC20500

How to Combine Two or More Fields

Step 1.   Move to a blank column (if you use a column that already contains a field name, you will have to clear it from the **Field** cell).

Step 2.   Select the column's **Field** cell.

Step 3.   Type the text you intend to use as the column heading.

Step 4.   Type a colon (:) to separate the column heading from your field list.

Step 5.   Type each field name, using either the ampersand (&) or the plus sign (+) to concatenate or add the field values, respectively.

Step 6.   If you need to separate field values with spaces or special characters, enclose them in quotes and add these between the field names. Remember to include an ampersand between all field names and quote-enclosed text.

If there is a syntax error in your field expression, Access will display a message that reads *The expression you entered contains invalid syntax.* The most common mistakes include failing to separate each component with an ampersand, not including a leading or trailing quote sign around spaces or special characters, not enclosing field names containing spaces with square brackets, or not spelling field names correctly.

If you misspell a field name Access will interpret it as a new parameter. When the query is run Access will prompt you with the misspelled field name. Return to **Query Design View** and correct the misspelling.

SQL Statements that Manipulate Fields

This chapter discussed four aspects of field manipulation: sorting, visibility, renaming, and combining two or more fields. Each of these actions has a SQL equivalent, although controlling field visibility has already been demonstrated - you simply omit the field name from the SQL field list (if the field is part of a criteria expression its name would appear in the WHERE clause).

Fields are either renamed or combined as part of the SQL field list. Ordering of the values in one or more fields is achieved by using the ORDER BY clause, which must follow the table name, and if present, any WHERE conditions.

The following table cites a few SQL examples of the operations conducted in this chapter.

SQL Statement	Description
SELECT tblStaffInfo.State, tblStaffInfo.City FROM tblStaffInfo ORDER BY tblStaffInfo.State;	Returns *City* and *State* values from table tblStaffInfo and orders the results by *State* alphabetical order.

SELECT tblStaffInfo.State,
   tblStaffInfo.City
FROM tblStaffInfo
ORDER BY tblStaffInfo.State,
   tblStaffInfo.City;
	As above but orders the results in the *City* field. The ordering is first by *State* and then by *City*. Example, Alabama addresses would appear first and within those rows the cities would appear A-Z, then Alaska with its cities ordered alphabetically.

SELECT tblStaffInfo.* FROM tblStaffInfo ORDER BY tblStaffInfo.StartDate DESC;	Returns all fields from table tblStaffInfo with the records ordered newest hires first (descending order is reverse order).
SELECT tblStaffInfo.City AS StaffCity, tblStaffInfo.State FROM tblStaffInfo;	Renames the *City* field as *StaffCity* and returns *StaffCity* and *State* field values from the table tblStaffInfo.
SELECT [FirstName] & " " & [LastName] AS FullName, tblStaffInfo.Department FROM tblStaffInfo;	Combines the *FirstName* and *LastName* fields (first placing a space between the two field values) and renaming the combined field *FullName*. Also returned is the *Department* field.

Chapter 5 | Function Expressions

Function expressions use built-in *functions* to perform some predefined task, such as adding or subtracting time to date values or finding the greatest value among a set of records. Once the function has returned a result, that value may be displayed as if it were a field value or used as part of a criteria expression.

Function expressions are used in one or two locations in the **Field Grid**.

- When placed in the Field row, function expressions are used to modify existing values. For example, a new column that contains the DateAdd() function could display a date 25 years greater than the employee's Start Date.

- When placed in a Criteria or Or row, a function expression is used to provide a value to a criteria. Only records that satisfy the criteria, as modified by the function, will be returned. For example, the DateDiff() function, when included in an expression in a Criteria row for the Start Date column could be used to locate all employees who started work within 12 days of a particular date.

- Function expressions may also be used in both the Field row and a Criteria or an Or row to create a new query field that uses a function to present calculated values and a function to limit the returned records.

You can create functions by typing directly in the appropriate **Field row** or **Criteria** or **Or** row, or by using the **Expression Builder**. This is a facility for selecting built-in functions and other expression elements. When finished, the **Expression Builder** can paste the expression into the current cell on the **Field Grid**.

Functions and Arguments

All functions return a value. For example, the function **Date()** returns the current date as specified by your computer's date/time settings. The empty parenthesis associated with the **Date** function indicates that the function does not require *arguments* in order to return a value. Many functions require one or more *arguments* to return some result. Arguments may be data to act upon, or may specify some parameter under which the function should operate. For example, the **LEFT** function returns a given number of characters from the left side of a string of text. This function takes two arguments. The first is the string to act upon and the second argument is the number of characters to return. As an example, **LEFT("Washington", 4)** would return the term *Wash*.

Points on Arguments

- A function may require no arguments, a single argument, or a list of several arguments. Functions referenced via the **Expression Builder** will include their argument list. On-line help may also be accessed to learn about a function's arguments.

- For multiple-argument functions, the arguments are separated from one another by commas, and the argument list is frequently referred to as a comma-delimited list.

- Some arguments are optional, although many are required. Generally, the optional arguments are placed toward the right end of an argument list. In on-line help, optional arguments are typically enclosed in square brackets [ ].

- On-line help is a useful resource for determining the specifics of a function and its argument list.

An example of a function that uses arguments is the **DateAdd** function. The syntax of this function appears as:

DateAdd (interval, number, date)

Argument	Description
Interval	The unit of time added. You can add any time unit (there are 10 available) including seconds (specified as "s"), hours("h"), days ("d"), weeks ("ww") or full years ("yyyy").
Number	The amount of time units to add.
Date	The date you wish to add time units to.

If you wished to add 25 years to the value in a field named *StartDate*, the function would appear as:

DateAdd ("yyyy", 25, [StartDate])

 All the arguments for the **DateAdd** function are required.

Expression Builder

The Expression Builder lets you construct expressions by browsing through lists of built-in functions, operators, and references to the objects in your database. The built-in functions and database objects are arranged categorically.

You can evoke the **Expression Builder** at any point when typing an expression anywhere in the **Field Grid**.

How to Work with the Expression Builder

Step 1.   Within the **Field Grid** select the desired cell.

Step 2.   If desired, begin typing the initial portion of an expression.

Step 3.   To start the **Expression Builder**, select the **Builder** button from the **Query Setup** group on the **Query Tools | Design** ribbon. The **Expression Builder** will appear similar to the following:

Components of the Expression Builder

Component	Description
Expression Box	Displays the expression as it is being built. You can directly enter text in this area or select **Operators** or items from the **Function List**.
Expression Elements	A list of the major categories of functions and objects available.
Expression Categories	Displays major categories associated with the currently selected item in the **Expression Element** list.
Expression Values	Lists all functions contained within the category selected in the **Categories** list. Double-clicking an item will insert it into the **Expression Box**.
Help Area	If an Expression Value is selected, a brief description of the function as well as it's argument list (if applicable) appears in the lower portion of the dialog box. The function name is a hyperlink and clicking on it opens on-line help for that function.

Step 4.   Select a major category from the **Expression Elements** list. If the target folder displays a plus (+) you must double-click on it to display subfolders.

Step 5.   From the **Categories** list select a category.

Step 6.   From the **Function List** select a function. Double-click on the function to insert it into the **Expression Box** or use the **Paste** button.

Step 7.   If arguments are required of the function, add them in the appropriate location within the function's *argument list*.

Step 8.   Continue with Steps 4 through 7 as required to continue building your expression.

Step 9.   Complete your expression and return to the **Query Design View** by choosing **OK**.

Function Categories

Category	Description
Arrays	Functions for determining array size.
Conversion	Functions that convert between data types.
Database	Tasks for creating database objects and obtaining system information.
Date/Time	General functions for manipulating date/time information.
Domain Aggregate	Tasks for providing statistical information about records in a recordset.
Error Handling	General error handling functions.
Financial	Functions for calculating a variety of financial tasks. These functions are a subset of those found in Microsoft Excel.
General	Generalized functions that do not easily fit into any of the other categories.
Inspection	Tasks to determine the state of a field value (such as whether it is empty or null).
Math	Standard mathematical functions.
Messages	Functions that will display input or message boxes.
Program Flow	Functions that can make decisions and control the overall flow of the expression.
SQL Aggregate	Similar to the **Domain Aggregate** functions, but part of the SQL language (the **Domain Aggregate** functions are not SQL-standard).
Text	General tasks for manipulating text data.

Common Functions

Name	Category	Description
Date()	Date/Time	Returns the system date.
DateAdd()	Date/Time	Adds a unit of time to a given date. You determine the type and amount of time units to add.
DateDiff()	Date/Time	Determines the time difference between two dates. Returns a value in any time unit you choose.
Time()	Date/Time	Returns the system time.
DAvg()	Domain Aggregate	Determines the average value from a field within a given table or query (also known as a *Domain*).
DCount()	Domain Aggregate	Returns the number of records within a table or query.
DLookup()	Domain Aggregate	Returns the contents of the **Expression** field in a domain. If no **Criteria** is used, the function returns a randomly found value. If two or more fields satisfy the **Criteria**, the first record found in the domain is used.
DMin(), DMax()	Domain Aggregate	Returns the smallest or largest value encountered in the **Expression** field of the domain.
DSum()	Domain Aggregate	Sums all values encountered in the **Expression** field of the domain.
IsEmpty	Inspection	Determines whether a field is empty.
IsNull	Inspection	Determines whether a field is null.
IIF	Program Flow	Evaluates an expression and returns one of two values (which themselves may be based on an expression), depending on whether the evaluation results in *True* or *False*.
Switch	Program Flow	Considers pairs of values; the first term in a pair is evaluated and the second term of the pair is returned if the evaluation is *True*.

How to Edit an Existing Expression Using the Expression Builder

Step 1.   Within the **Field Grid** select the desired cell.

Step 2.   From the **Query Setup** group select **Builder**.

Step 3.   Use the **Expression Builder** to edit the expression.

Step 4.   Choose **OK**.

You can also edit an expression directly in its containing cell, or place the insertion point in the cell and press *Shift* + *F2* to open the **Zoom** window.

Examples of Function Expressions

There are many ways to use functions in expressions. This section will present a series of examples, arranged according to the overall task.

Keep in mind that a function expression located in a **Field** row of the **Field Grid** will serve to supply data to that field. Placing a function expression in either the **Criteria** or the **Or** row means that the function will provide data for a criteria to limit the records returned.

Functions that Return Values

This category includes functions that return some value for use in creating a new field or for establishing criteria. These examples use two different functions, **DateAdd** and **DateDiff**, and the following explains the syntax for each function.

Syntax: DateAdd(interval, amount, date) Using the *interval* (which can be any unit of time such as seconds, quarters, or years) adds the *amount* to the *date*.

As an example, if you needed to create a new calculated field in a query that determines when a report is due (say 45 days from the *ProjectEndDate* field value) you would enter the following text in a blank Field cell:

ReportDue: DateAdd("d" , 45, [ProjectEndDate])

When the query is run, the column named **ReportDue** will present date values, each 45 days beyond the **ProjectEndDate** value for that record. The criteria grid for such an example may appear similar to the following:

Field:	ProjectName	ProjectStartDate	ProjectEndDate	ReportDue: DateAdd("d",45,[ProjectEndDate])
Table:	tblProjects	tblProjects	tblProjects	
Sort:				
Show:	☑	☑	☑	☑
Criteria:				
or:				

When the query is run the **Datasheet View** would appear similar to the following:

ProjectName	ProjectStartDate	ProjectEndDate	ReportDue
Server upgrade	9/15/2014	11/30/2014	1/14/2015
Website upgrade	10/1/2011	12/31/2011	2/14/2012
VOIP migration	10/1/2014	10/10/2014	11/24/2014
Financial System Reengineering	10/1/2013	12/31/2013	2/14/2014
Marketing Survey	6/1/2013	9/30/2013	11/14/2013
Six Sigma Implementation	1/2/2012	12/30/2012	2/13/2013
Cloud Storage Implementation	2/1/2014		

Syntax: DateDiff(interval, date1, date2) Given the *interval* (any valid unit of time), determine the number of interval units between date1 and date2.

As an example, say you needed to filter a query based on projects that ended less than 30 days ago. You would enter the following text into the **Criteria** cell in the *ProjectEndDate* column:

DateDiff("d", [ProjectEndDate], Date()) < 30

Functions that Make Decisions

Functions in this group are capable of controlling the outcome of an expression based on how some test condition is evaluated. The most common decision-making functions are immediate If (IIF) and Switch.

Syntax: IIF(test condition, true part, false part) Given a *test condition* return *true part* if the expression is true, otherwise return *false part*.

As an example, say your query contains a field **Gender** that contains either **M** or **F**. You would like to substitute those terms in your query results with either **Male** or **Female** instead. The syntax, added in a **Field** cell would appear as:

Gender: IIF([Gender]="F", "Female", "Male")

The *test condition* is whether the data in any given row contains the value *F*. If it does the function returns *Female*, otherwise the function returns *Male*.

For another example, consider the need to note whether a project is considered **Short term** or **Long term** if the difference between the ProjectStartDate and ProjectEndDate fields is more than 30 days. You would place the following term in a blank **Field** cell in order to create a new column named *ProjectTerm*:

ProjectTerm: IIf(DateDiff("d", [ProjectStartDate], [ProjectEndDate]) > 30,"Short Term", "Long Term")

The example above, entered into the criteria grid of a query might appear similar to:

Field:	ProjectName	ProjectStartDate	ProjectEndDate	ProjectTerm: IIf(DateDiff("d",[ProjectStartDate],[ProjectEndDate])>30,"Short Term","Long Term")
Table:	tblProjects	tblProjects	tblProjects	
Sort:				
Show:	☑	☑	☑	☑
Criteria:				
or:				

And the results displayed in **Datasheet View** may appear as:

ProjectName ▾	ProjectStartDate ▾	ProjectEndDate ▾	ProjectTerm ▾
Server upgrade	9/15/2014	11/30/2014	Short Term
Website upgrade	10/1/2011	12/31/2011	Short Term
VOIP migration	10/1/2014	10/10/2014	Long Term
Financial System Reengineering	10/1/2013	12/31/2013	Short Term
Marketing Survey	6/1/2013	9/30/2013	Short Term
Six Sigma Implementation	1/2/2012	12/30/2012	Short Term
Cloud Storage Implementation	2/1/2014		Long Term

If you placed the criteria = *"Short Term"* in the criteria cell for the *ProjectTerm* column only short term projects would appear in the final results.

Syntax: Switch(Expression1, Value1 [,Expression2, Value2] [,Expression3, Value3]…)
Here the square brackets indicate that additional expression, value pairs are optional and are not part of the syntax for the function.

As an example, you need to add an additional column to a query named **Language** that lists the official language given the value of the **County** field in your query. Located in a **Field** cell the syntax would appear similar to the following:

Language: Switch([Country]="Brazil", "Portuguese", [Country]="Peru", "Spanish", [Country]="Aruba", "Dutch")

The square brackets used in the example above denote that **County** is a field elsewhere in the query.

The example above, formatted in the criteria grid of a query would appear as:

Field:	Country	Language: Switch([Country]="Brazil","Portuguese",[Country]="Peru","Spanish",[Country]="Aruba","Dutch")
Table:	tblVolunteers	
Sort:		
Show:	☑	☑
Criteria:		
or:		

And the **Datasheet** view would appear similar to the following:

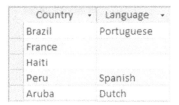

Country	·	Language	·
Brazil		Portuguese	
France			
Haiti			
Peru		Spanish	
Aruba		Dutch	

Expressions Using Domain Aggregate Functions

The Domain Aggregate functions are unique in that they can summarize or gather information from another record source (also called a *Domain*). Domain Aggregate functions are used like other functions to specify criteria or create calculated fields. The Domain Aggregate functions are listed in the table below.

Domain Aggregate Functions

Option	Description
DAvg	Finds the average value over the specified domain.
DCount	Counts the number of values (records) within the domain.
DFirst, DLast	Finds the first or last field in a domain, respectively.
DLookup	Retrieves the value of a specified field from a set of records.
DMin, DMax	Finds the minimum or maximum value in a domain, respectively.
DStDev, DStDevP	Returns the estimated standard deviation of a population sample or of a population, respectively.
DSum	Calculates the sum of all field values over the given domain.
DVar, DVarP	Returns the estimated variance of a population sample or of a population, respectively.

All domain aggregate functions take the same argument list:

Syntax: Dname (field name, table name, [optional where condition])

The *field name* is the name of the field of interest, contained in the table denoted in *table name*. The *where condition* is optimal and is used to restrict the records that the domain aggregate function acts upon.

One common domain aggregate function is **Dmax** which finds the largest value within the specified field. For example, to find the highest budget for any staff on a project you may create a field expression similar to the following:

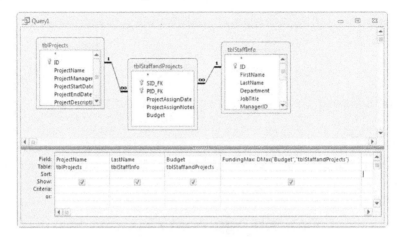

And the results from such a query would appear similar to the following:

ProjectName	LastName	Budget	FundingMax
Server upgrade	Kidwell	$40,000.00	95000
Server upgrade	Palmer	$7,500.00	95000
Server upgrade	Jones	$3,000.00	95000
Server upgrade	Regal	$500.00	95000
Server upgrade	Jones	$500.00	95000
Website upgrade	Palmer	$4,000.00	95000
Website upgrade	Michaels	$4,000.00	95000
Website upgrade	Green	$500.00	95000
Website upgrade	Regal	$1,000.00	95000
Website upgrade	Link	$2,000.00	95000
Website upgrade	Rosa	$2,000.00	95000
VOIP migration	Kidwell	$30,000.00	95000
VOIP migration	Smith	$10,000.00	95000
VOIP migration	Regal	$10,000.00	95000
VOIP migration	De Haven	$7,500.00	95000
VOIP migration	DeLuca	$7,500.00	95000

The repeating value in the **FundingMax** column may seem odd but the domain aggregate function is performing as expected. It does not act on individual row values like the functions discussed earlier. In this case, **DMax** has located the maximum value in the **budget** field in the **tblStaffandProjects** table.

Usually, Domain Aggregate functions are used to provide data to a greater expression. In this case, if the example above were modified to take the budget amount for each staff/project combination and express it as a percentage of the greatest budget amount the expression in the **FundingMax** cell would appear as:

PercentOfMax: [Budget]/DMax("Budget","tblStaffandProjects")

And the resulting data would appear similar to the following:

ProjectName	LastName	Budget	PercentOfMax
Server upgrade	Kidwell	$40,000.00	42.11%
Server upgrade	Palmer	$7,500.00	7.89%
Server upgrade	Jones	$3,000.00	3.16%
Server upgrade	Regal	$500.00	0.53%
Server upgrade	Jones	$500.00	0.53%
Website upgrade	Palmer	$4,000.00	4.21%
Website upgrade	Michaels	$4,000.00	4.21%
Website upgrade	Green	$500.00	0.53%
Website upgrade	Regal	$1,000.00	1.05%
Website upgrade	Link	$2,000.00	2.11%
Website upgrade	Rosa	$2,000.00	2.11%
VOIP migration	Kidwell	$30,000.00	31.58%
VOIP migration	Smith	$10,000.00	10.53%
VOIP migration	Regal	$10,000.00	10.53%
VOIP migration	De Haven	$7,500.00	7.89%
VOIP migration	DeLuca	$7,500.00	7.89%

There are cases where a Domain Aggregate function is useful as part of a criteria expression. Looking at the data from above, if you needed to list staff who have budgets less than the average budget, you would enter the following expression in the **criteria** cell of the **Budget** column:

<DAvg("Budget","tblStaffandProjects")

In the **Design View** it would appear similar to:

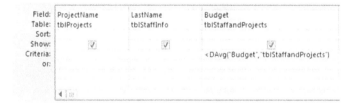

And the result set would appear as:

ProjectName	LastName	Budget
Server upgrade	Palmer	$7,500.00
Server upgrade	Jones	$3,000.00
Server upgrade	Regal	$500.00
Server upgrade	Jones	$500.00
Website upgrade	Palmer	$4,000.00
Website upgrade	Michaels	$4,000.00
Website upgrade	Green	$500.00
Website upgrade	Regal	$1,000.00
Website upgrade	Link	$2,000.00
Website upgrade	Rosa	$2,000.00
VOIP migration	Smith	$10,000.00
VOIP migration	Regal	$10,000.00
VOIP migration	De Haven	$7,500.00
VOIP migration	DeLuca	$7,500.00

C5 Domain Aggregate 2

 Aggregate functions vary widely between various relational database systems. Microsoft Access is unique in using functions that specify field and table names *within* the function. The ANSI and ISO SQL standard specifies far fewer functions (AVG, SUM, MIN, MAX, COUNT) which use a syntax which is different from the Domain Aggregate functions discussed here.

SQL Function Statements

Functions differ greatly between various database implementations and Microsoft Access is no exception. Many functions listed in the **Expression Builder,** including the Domain Aggregate Functions, are not part of the SQL language specification so care should be taken if creating queries that use expressions where you intend on porting the query to another database system.

In general, when you implement a Microsoft Access function within the **Query Design View** it appears similarly constructed in **SQL** view. Functions placed in any of the **Field** cells will end up in the Field List in the SQL statement, while functions placed in any **Criteria** cell will be associated with the **WHERE** clause.

Chapter 6 | Totals Queries

Totals queries are queries that use an *aggregate* function to produce a sum, count, average value, or some other summary operation in one or more fields. The queries that can be converted into totals queries are select, append, crosstab, and make table queries. A totals query is created by selecting the **Totals** command when working in **Query Design View**. A new row, *Total*, appears in the **Field Grid**. Each cell in the **Total** row can display a drop-down list that lists the nine aggregate functions and three additional functions that can be applied to the query. .

A totals query differs from using domain aggregate functions as discussed in the previous chapter in that totals queries always group data. When you create a totals query in Microsoft Access it is the same as using the SQL standard GROUP BY clause.

A special subset of a totals query, the **Crosstab Query**, will be discussed in Chapter 9.

Points on Totals Queries

- At least one field in a totals query must have an aggregate function applied.

- If all the fields in a query have an aggregate function applied, the query will display a single row in Datasheet view. Each cell will contain the results of whichever aggregate function was applied to that field. There will be no grouping in this type of query.

- If at least one field in a totals query has the **Group by** option applied, and at least one field has an aggregate function, the query will group the results of the aggregate function. This is a useful method of producing totals arranged within groups.

- Fields with null values are ignored by the aggregate functions. For example, records with a null value in the field containing an aggregate function such as **Count** will not be counted.

- There are 12 options in the drop-down list that appears in any given Totals cell in the Field Grid. Nine of these are aggregate functions; the remaining three are additional options. Both sets of options are outlined in this section.

- When you apply an aggregate function to a query field, the field's name is modified. Access combines the aggregate function name, the word *Of* and the original field name to create the new field name. As an example, applying the **Avg** aggregate function to the *Budget* field will result in the field name *AvgOfBudget*.

How to Create a Totals Query (Generalized Procedure)

Step 1.   Open an existing query in **Query Design View** or start a new query.

Step 2.   Add the desired fields to the **Field Grid**.

Step 3.   Select the **Totals** button from the **Show/Hide** group of the **Tools** ribbon.

Step 4.   Select the **Total** cell for the desired field.

Step 5.   From the drop-down list, choose the appropriate **Aggregate Function** or **Summary Option**. Use the following two tables as a guide.

Aggregate Functions

Name	Description	Applicable Data Type
Sum	Totals all the values in the field.	Number, Date/Time, Currency, and AutoNumber.
Avg	Returns the average value from the values in the field.	Number, Date/Time, Currency, and AutoNumber.
Max, Min	Lists the highest or lowest value in a field. In a text field, returns the first or last value as sorted alphabetically.	Text, Number, Date/Time, Currency, and AutoNumber.
Count	Counts the number of records that contain non-null data in the field.	Text, Memo, Number, Date/Time, Currency, AutoNumber, Yes/No, and OLE Object.
StDev	Standard deviation of the values in a field.	Number, Date/Time, Currency, and AutoNumber.
Var	Variance (square of the standard deviation) of the values in a field.	Number, Date/Time, Currency, and AutoNumber.

 Two additional functions, *First* and *Last*, will return the field value in the first or last record in the table, respectively. Their natural order, or the order in which they were entered into the database, determines the first and last records. This order is independent of any sorting or indexing applied and is therefore of limited value.

Summary Options

Option	Description
Group By	Define the field or fields you wish to group. For example, to show total employees per project, use **Group By** in the *ProjectName* field and the **Count** function in the *EmployeeID* field (or a field that uniquely identifies an employee).
Expression	If you add a calculated field that includes one or more aggregate functions in its expression, you must set the calculated field's **Total** cell to *Expression*. If you fail to do this, Access will respond with an error message.
Where	Specify criteria for a field that is not participating in the grouping or summary fields. If you select this option for a field, Access will hide the field in the query results by clearing the **Show** check box.

Step 6.   Repeat Steps 4 and 5, as desired to set Aggregate Functions or Summary Options for other fields.

Step 7.   Run the query by switching to **Datasheet View**.

Step 8.   If desired, save the query design.

How to Create a Simple Totals Query

This procedure will create a query that will perform one or more **Aggregate Functions** on each of the query fields. No grouping is applied and therefore only a single record is returned.

Step 1.   Open an existing query in **Query Design View** or start a new query.

Step 2.   Add the desired fields to the **Field Grid**.

Step 3.   From the **Query Design** toolbar select the **Totals** button, or, from the **View** menu choose **Totals**.

Step 4.   Select the **Total** cell for the desired field.

Step 5.   From the drop-down box, choose the appropriate **Aggregate Function.** Refer to the table on page 54 to check that the selected function is appropriate for the field's data type.

Step 6.   Repeat Steps 4 and 5 for all the query fields.

Step 7.   Run the query by switching to **Datasheet View**.

As an example, a query that sums **project budgets** and also presents the smallest and largest amount budgeted to a project would appear as follows in **Query Design View**:

Field:	Budget	Budget	Budget
Table:	tblStaffandProjects	tblStaffandProjects	tblStaffandProjects
Total:	Sum	Min	Max
Sort:			
Show:	☑	☑	☑
Criteria:			
or:			

When the query is run by changing to **Datasheet View**, the results would appear similar to the following:

Query1		
SumOfBudget ▾	MinOfBudget ▾	MaxOfBudget ▾
$444,500.00	$500.00	$95,000.00

How to Create a Grouped Totals Query

This procedure will create a query that will perform one or more **Aggregate Functions** on the selected query fields. At least one field must have its **Totals** cell set to *Group by*.

Step 1.   Open an existing query in **Query Design View** or start a new query.

Step 2.   Add the desired fields to the **Field Grid**.

Step 3.   From the **Query Design** toolbar select the **Totals** button, or, from the **View** menu choose **Totals**.

Step 4.   Select the **Total** cell for the desired field, which will have an **Aggregate Function** applied.

Step 5.   From the drop-down list, choose the appropriate **Aggregate Function.** Refer to the table on page 54 to check that the selected function is appropriate for the field's data type.

Step 6.   Repeat Steps 4 and 5 for other fields, as necessary.

Step 7.   Ensure that the field or fields you wish to group by have their **Totals** cell set to the **Group by** option.

Step 8.   Run the query by switching to **Datasheet View**.

As an example, a query that tallies individual staff budgets and groups them against *Project name* would appear similar to the following in **Query Design View**:

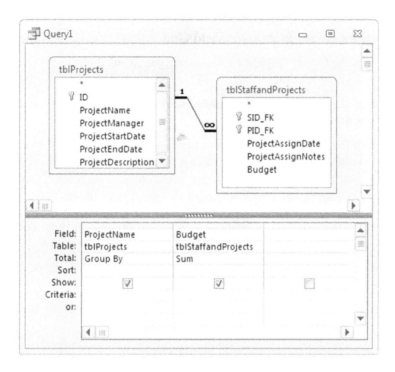

When this query is run by changing to **Datasheet View**, the results would appear similar to the following:

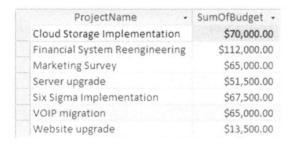

ProjectName	SumOfBudget
Cloud Storage Implementation	$70,000.00
Financial System Reengineering	$112,000.00
Marketing Survey	$65,000.00
Server upgrade	$51,500.00
Six Sigma Implementation	$67,500.00
VOIP migration	$65,000.00
Website upgrade	$13,500.00

How to Create a Totals Query that Uses Criteria

Fields that supply criteria values in a totals query have their **Total** cell set to *Where*. These fields are not displayed in the results nor do they provide data for the summary. If you wish to show field values from such a field, you must add it twice to the **Field Grid**. For the duplicate field, set its **Total** cell to one of the **Aggregate Functions** or to **Group by**.

Step 1.   Open an existing query in **Query Design View** or start a new query.

Step 2.   Add the desired fields to the **Field Grid**.

Step 3.   From the **Query Design** toolbar select the **Totals** button, or, from the **View** menu choose **Totals**.

Step 4.   Select the **Total** cell for the desired field, which will have an **Aggregate Function** applied.

Step 5.   From the drop-down list, choose the appropriate **Aggregate Function.** Refer to the table on page 54. to check that the selected function is appropriate for the field's data type.

Step 6.   Repeat Steps 4 and 5 for other fields, as necessary.

Step 7.   Ensure that the field or fields you wish to group by have their **Totals** cell set to the **Group by** option.

Step 8.   Select the **Total** cell for a field which will use a criteria expression and from the drop-down list, choose **Where**.

Step 9.   In the **Criteria** cell type an expression or use the **Expression Builder** to create an expression.

Step 10.   Run the query by switching to **Datasheet View**.

As an example, taking the previous query we'll add a condition to only return totals for projects that are ongoing – e.g. their ProjectEndDate value is *Null* In **Query Design View** it would appear as:

Field:	ProjectName	Budget	ProjectEndDate
Table:	tblProjects	tblStaffandProjects	tblProjects
Total:	Group By	Sum	Where
Sort:			
Show:	✓	✓	☐
Criteria:			Is Null
or:			

When this query is run by changing to **Datasheet View**, the results would appear similar to the following:

ProjectName	SumOfBudget
Cloud Storage Implementation	$70,000.00

If you need to apply a criteria to one of the fields whose total value is either **Group By** or is one of the aggregate functions, you simply apply the criteria to the appropriate **Criteria** cell for that column. For example, to sum the budget of projects that have the term *upgrade* in the project name, the criteria grid would appear similar to the following:

Field:	ProjectName	Budget
Table:	tblProjects	tblStaffandProjects
Total:	Group By	Sum
Sort:		
Show:	☑	☑
Criteria:	Like "*upgrade*"	
or:		

When viewed in **Datasheet View** the results would appear as:

ProjectName	SumOfBudget
Server upgrade	$51,500.00
Website upgrade	$13,500.00

How to Create a Totals Query that Uses an Expression

The *Expression* option in the **Totals** cell is used when you need to create a new field to display results of an expression. In a totals query, expressions must involve an aggregate function such as **Sum()** or **Avg()**.

Step 1.   Open an existing query in **Query Design View** or start a new query.

Step 2.   Add the desired fields to the **Field Grid**.

Step 3.   From the **Query Design** toolbar select the **Totals** button, or, from the **View** menu choose **Totals**.

Step 4.   Specify aggregate functions, grouping, and/or criteria expressions for fields.

Step 5.   Select the first blank field in the **Field Grid**.

Step 6.   In the **Total** cell, select the drop-down list and choose **Expression**.

Step 7.   In the **Field** cell, type a new field name followed by a colon (:), then type an expression (or use the **Expression Builder**).

Step 8.   Run the query by switching to **Datasheet View**.

Continuing with the previous examples, if you wanted to tally the total budget for each project *and* include a calculated field (an expression) that projected each project's total budget by 20%, the expression in a new **Field** cell would appear as:

Field:	ProjectName	Budget	Inflation: [SumofBudget]*1.2 ▾
Table:	tblProjects	tblStaffandProjects	
Total:	Group By	Sum	Expression
Sort:			
Show:	☑	☑	☑
Criteria:			
or:			

When the query is run by changing to **Datasheet View**, the results would appear similar to the following:

ProjectName ▾	SumOfBudget ▾	Inflation ▾
Cloud Storage Implementation	$70,000.00	$84,000.00
Financial System Reengineering	$112,000.00	$134,400.00
Marketing Survey	$65,000.00	$78,000.00
Server upgrade	$51,500.00	$61,800.00
Six Sigma Implementation	$67,500.00	$81,000.00
VOIP migration	$65,000.00	$78,000.00
Website upgrade	$13,500.00	$16,200.00

In the example above, note that the expression referred to the field *SumOfBudget* rather than to *Budget* (the actual name of the field). When you refer to a field in a totals query and the field has an aggregate function applied you must refer to the field as Access will name it. In this case the field *Budget* is retitled *SumOfBudget* as a result of the **Sum** operator being applied to that field. If in doubt about field naming, switch the query to **DataSheet View** to see how Access will name the desired field.

SQL Statements that Total and Group

In a manner similar to Microsoft Access functions, the totals functions constitute a list larger than that of the general SQL language specification. Of the totals functions in Access, only AVG(), COUNT(), FIRST(), LAST(), MAX(), MIN(), and SUM() are universally understood by database management systems.

Like function expressions (discussed in Chapter 5) that operate on a field (as opposed to being part of a criteria expression), totals functions are manifest as part of the field list in a select query. This makes sense as the function is used to transform the values of the field.

Grouping of results in a totals query involves a separate clause, **GROUP BY**. If a totals query includes a criteria expression and groups, the **WHERE** clause is replaced by the **HAVING** clause, which precedes the **GROUP BY** keyword pair. This is a standard condition in SQL.

The following table cites a few SQL examples that total and/or group.

SQL Statement	Description
SELECT Sum(tblStaffandProjects.Budget) AS SumOfBudget, Min(tblStaffandProjects.Budget) AS MinOfBudget, Max(tblStaffandProjects.Budget) AS MaxOfBudget FROM tblStaffandProjects;	Creates three fields, one that totals all budget records, a second that lists the smallest budget field value and a third that lists the largest budget field value for all records in the tblStaffandProjects table.
SELECT tblProjects.ProjectName, Sum(tblStaffandProjects.Budget) AS SumOfBudget FROM tblProjects INNER JOIN tblStaffandProjects ON tblProjects.ID = tblStaffandProjects.PID_FK GROUP BY tblProjects.ProjectName;	Sums all budget field values in the tblStaffandProjects table, grouped by ProjectName (from the tblProjects table).
SELECT tblProjects.ProjectName, Sum(tblStaffandProjects.Budget) AS SumOfBudget FROM tblProjects INNER JOIN tblStaffandProjects ON tblProjects.ID = tblStaffandProjects.PID_FK GROUP BY tblProjects.ProjectName HAVING (((tblProjects.ProjectName) Like "*web*"));	As above except it only sums and groups by projects with the term *web* contained in the project name.

Chapter 7 | Join Properties

A *join* is a way of relating the records in one table to those in another table when constructing a query. Joins are related to *relationships* because, by default, adding two related tables (as defined in the **Relationships** window) to a query will automatically set the join properties to the default *equi-join*. Access recognizes three join types, which are discussed below.

Points on Join Properties

▪ By default, unless a join is set otherwise in the **Relationships** window, all joins in a relational database are specified as equi-joins.

▪ Modifying join properties in a query does not affect the join properties in the **Relationships** window. In fact, modifying query joins is the preferred method of handling those situations where special join properties are required. A join specified in a query remains as part of the query's definition and does not affect joins as specified in the **Relationships** window.

▪ The terms *left* and *right* join come from the habit of drawing or placing the table constituting the one side of a relationship join to the left and placing or drawing the table constituting the many side of the join on the right.

Equi-Join

This join type is the most common. It connects two tables, usually related by a one-to-many relationship, and displays all records in the *one* side of the join that contain related records in the *many* side of the join.

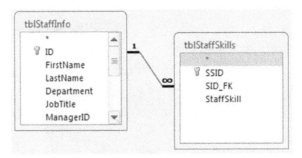

For example, in the illustration above staff records are related to a table containing staff skill information. This represents the situation where one employee may have *many* work skills. If you produced an *equi-join* query that listed employee first and last names, and their work skills, then the query would only list those employees who have at least one skill in the staff skills table.

Employees lacking any listed work skills will not appear in the result. The following example illustrates this point.

Consider two tables, **Employees** and **Skills**, which are related by a one-to-many join:

Table: Employees			Tables Joined	Table: Skills	
Staff (PK)	**Office**		**One to Many**	**Staff (FK)**	**Skill**
Mary	CB 200			Mary	Mediation
John	CB 210			Mary	Facilitation
Tonya	CB 355			Tonya	Budgeting
				Tonya	Facilitation
PK: *Primary Key*				Tonya	Planning
FK: *Foreign Key*					Web design

In a query using an equi-join, only records are displayed when there are matches between the primary and foreign key fields in both tables. **This is the default join type.** The results of a query based on an equi-join would appear as:

Staff	**Office**	**Skill**
Mary	CB 200	Mediation
Mary	CB 200	Facilitation
Tonya	CB 355	Budgeting
Tonya	CB 355	Facilitation
Tonya	CB 355	Planning

Note that because *John* lacks any listed work skills, he does not appear in the query results. Also, since there is a skill, *Web design* that isn't associated with a staff member it also does not appear in the query results. A record on the many side of a one-to-many relationship that lacks a corresponding record on the one side is called *orphaned data*. Usually orphaned data violate rules of referential integrity.

Left Join

Left joins include *all* records from the table representing the *one* side of the relationship join and only those records from the table representing the *many* side of the join where there is a match.

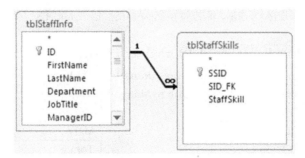

Using the previous sample tables as a guide, the same query, originally run using an equi-join but now configured to use a left join, would yield these results:

Staff	Office	Skill
Mary	CB 200	Mediation
Mary	CB 200	Facilitation
Tonya	CB 355	Budgeting
Tonya	CB 355	Facilitation
Tonya	CB 355	Planning
John	CB 210	

Note that John now appears in the query results regardless of the status of his skill records. As with the equi-join however, the orphaned *Web design* skill still fails to appear in the query results.

 Left joins are common when producing reports where you need to include all records from a table on the one side of a join, and only those records from the many side of the join when there is a match between the tables.

Right Join

Right joins include *all* records from the table representing the *many* side of the relationship join and only those records from the table representing the *one* side of the join where there is a match. This join type is rarely used as its general purpose is to locate *orphaned data* from the table containing the *many* records. In a relational database with referential integrity established, this condition cannot exist. Right joins are frequently used when troubleshooting the importation of data from other sources or when working with a database that did not have referential integrity enforced.

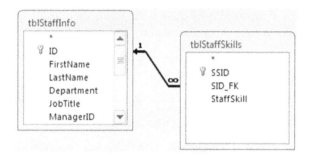

Using the sample tables on page 63 as a guide, the same query, originally run using an equi-join but now configured to use a right join, would yield these results:

Staff	Office	Skill
Mary	CB 200	Mediation
Mary	CB 200	Facilitation
Tonya	CB 355	Budgeting
Tonya	CB 355	Facilitation
Tonya	CB 355	Planning
		Web design

Note that a record exists for a skill that is not associated with anyone from the **Employees** table. This represents an *orphaned record.* The last record could be deleted from the query **Datasheet.**

 Right joins are rarely used in a relational database that enforces referential integrity. Their primary purpose is to identify orphaned records in tables on the many side of a join, especially when importing data from other data sources, or if the relational database was set to not enforce referential integrity.

Managing Joins

As discussed above, there are situations where you need to modify an existing join property, or add or remove a join between two tables. Modifying joins in a query does not affect joins in the **Relationships** window. Query joins are saved with the design of the query.

You must be in **Query Design View** to modify query joins graphically. Joins are established as part of the query's SQL statement. Unless you are familiar with SQL syntax, it is not recommended that you modify join properties using the **SQL View**.

How to Create a Join

There are good reasons for creating a join for a query and not necessarily establishing that same join in the **Relationships** window. Chapter 8 details several of these.

Step 1. If the desired tables and/or queries are not present in the **Table Area**, add them. Refer to page 9 for instructions.

Step 2. Working in the **Table Area**, position the mouse pointer over the field in one table or query that you wish to join with the field in another table or query.

Step 3. Drag the mouse pointer from the one table or query to the other table or query.

Step 4. Release the mouse over the destination field.

Step 5. Adjust join properties if desired. The following procedure discusses this topic.

How to Modify an Existing Join

Step 1. In **Query Design View** locate the desired join and double-click. A dialog box similar to the following will appear:

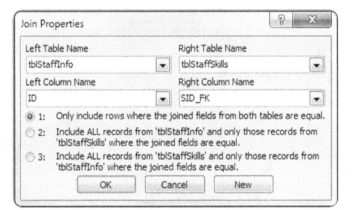

When attempting to double-click on a thin object such as a join line, point using the extreme arrow tip of the mouse cursor.

Step 2. Adjust the join type as desired.

Option	Description
Left/Right Table Name	Changes the table that is on either the left or right side of the join. By convention, a table on the *left* side contains the primary key when two tables are related in a one-to-many join.
Left/Right Column Name	Changes the field in the left or right table that the join is based on.
Join Option 1	This creates an equi-join, which is the default in most relational joins. Only matching records from both tables are displayed.
Join Option 2	Creates a left join. All records from the left table (the *one* side) and only those from the right table (the *many* side) that have matching records.
Join Option 3	Creates a right join. All records from the right table (the *many* side) and only those records from the left table (the *one* side) that have matching records.
New	Creates an entirely new join between any two tables or queries listed in the **Table Area**.

Step 3. Choose **OK**.

The type of join will be indicated graphically. An arrow-shaped join from one-to-many represents a left join, an arrow-shaped join from the many side to the one side represents a right join, and a join without arrows represents an equi-join.

Step 4. Continue modifying the query design if desired and then run it to verify the results.

Step 5. If desired, save the query. The modified join will be saved with the query design.

How to Remove a Join

Step 1. In **Query Design View** locate the desired join and click on it.

When attempting to double-click on a thin object such as a join line, point using the extreme arrow tip of the mouse cursor

Step 2. Press *Delete*.

How to Save a Join

Saving a join defined in a query only affects the query. It does not affect any joins as defined in the **Relationships** window.

Step 1.   From the **Quick Access** toolbar, select the **Save** button, or, choose **Save** when you close the query design or datasheet view.

SQL Join Statements

For each of the three join types discussed above there are equivalent statements in SQL. If we consider two tables connected by an *equi-join* as illustrated below:

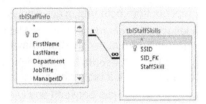

The SQL statement underlying a query that would display FirstName and LastName from the tblStaffInfo table and StaffSkills from the tblStaffStills table would appear as:

SELECT tblStaffInfo.FirstName, tblStaffInfo.LastName, tblStaffSkills.StaffSkill

FROM tblStaffInfo **INNER JOIN** tblStaffSkills **ON** tblStaffInfo.ID = tblStaffSkills.SID_FK;

The join syntax takes the form INNER JOIN [primary key table] ON [primary key field]=[foreign key table].[foreign key field].

If the join were modified to become a *left join*, as illustrated below:

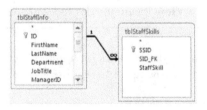

The SQL statement would appear as:

SELECT tblStaffInfo.FirstName, tblStaffInfo.LastName, tblStaffSkills.StaffSkill

FROM tblStaffInfo **LEFT JOIN** tblStaffSkills **ON** tblStaffInfo.ID = tblStaffSkills.SID_FK;

The difference being that the reserved word LEFT is used to modify the JOIN directive.

Likewise, modifying the original query to create a *right join* would appear as followings in **Query Design View**:

And the underlying SQL statement would appear as:

SELECT tblStaffInfo.FirstName, tblStaffInfo.LastName, tblStaffSkills.StaffSkill

FROM tblStaffInfo **RIGHT JOIN** tblStaffSkills **ON** tblStaffInfo.ID = tblStaffSkills.SID_FK;

The JOIN directive being modified by the presence of the RIGHT keyword.

Microsoft Access does not fully implement the SQL standard for joins, although equi-, left- and right-joins are the most common types.

Chapter 8 | Special Join Types

In this chapter we discuss a few special case queries. Self joins are used when a table contains a field that references another field in the same table. Theta joins let you ask questions of *inequality* between datasets and are useful for quality control and research purposes. Finally we'll address how to ask a type of question where you wish to find multiple values in the same column. There are three approaches to this last issue and we will explore each in detail.

Self-Joins

Self-joins are used when a field in a table contains information from another field in the same table. An example is an *Employees* table that has a field named *ManagerID*. Since managers are also employees, this is a common way to link employees to their managers. In the example below, the ManagerID field stores the *EmployeeID* number for each employee's manager. Note that in this table the primary key is the *EmployeeID* field.

An example of a table set up in this manner is illustrated below.

ID	FirstName	LastName	ManagerID	StartDate
8	Amanda	Smith	18	9/23/2005
9	Robert	Jones	8	8/14/2007
10	Tonya	Green	8	5/3/2007
11	Michael	McDonald	8	10/14/2000
12	Leon	DeLuca	15	9/1/2005
13	John	Michaels	15	12/14/2003
14	Susan	Palmer	15	2/8/2007
15	Michael	Kidwell	18	5/22/2004
16	Jennifer	Jones	15	6/2/2009
17	Tyrone	Baseman	15	5/17/2010
18	Greg	Oltman		11/4/2000
19	Cindy	Regal	18	10/19/2003
20	Mary	Wiseman	21	4/30/2006
21	John	Ramsey	18	7/9/2010

To create a query that would list the names of each employee's manager, you would create a query with a self-join.

How to Create a Self-Join in a Query (Generalized Procedure)

Step 1.   Create a select query. When the **Show Tables** dialog box is visible, add the target table twice. Close the **Show Tables** dialog when done. Note that the second copy of the table will have _*1* appended to its name.

Step 2.   Add the desired fields from the first copy of the table to the **Field Grid**.

Step 3.   To create the self-join, drag the mouse pointer from the field in the original table to its corresponding field in the copy of the table. **Example:** from *ManagerID* in the first table to *EmployeeID* in the copy of the first table.

The **Query Design View** in such a query would appear similar to the following:

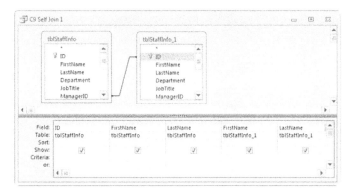

Step 4.   Add the desired fields from the second copy of the table. In this example it would be the *FirstName* and *LastName* fields which will correspond to the manager's first and last name.

Step 5.   If you wish to include the managers (or any employees with a *ManagerID* field that is empty - in other words a *left join*), set the join property by double-clicking on it and choosing the option **Include all records from (original table name) and only those records from (copy table name) where the joined fields are equal.** Choose **OK**.

Step 6.   Run the query by changing to **Datasheet View**. The results of a query with a self-join will appear similar to the following:

ID	tblStaffIr	tblStaffInfo.	tblStaffInfo	tblStaffInfo
18	Greg	Oltman		
9	Robert	Jones	Amanda	Smith
10	Tonya	Green	Amanda	Smith
11	Michael	McDonald	Amanda	Smith
12	Leon	DeLuca	Michael	Kidwell
13	John	Michaels	Michael	Kidwell
14	Susan	Palmer	Michael	Kidwell
16	Jennifer	Jones	Michael	Kidwell
17	Tyrone	Baseman	Michael	Kidwell
8	Amanda	Smith	Greg	Oltman
15	Michael	Kidwell	Greg	Oltman
19	Cindy	Regal	Greg	Oltman
21	John	Ramsey	Greg	Oltman

In the example above, you could establish an expression to combine the first and last name of each manager into a single new field, *Manager Name*. Note, however, that Access cannot tell from which table the *FirstName* and *LastName* fields are referring to. In this case, you must use the syntax, *[Table Name].[Field Name]*, to make the expression unambiguous. The full syntax for such an expression, located in the **Field** cell of a new column, would appear as:

Manager: [tblStaffInso_1].[FirstName] & " " & [tblStaffInfo_1].[LastName]

The results of such an expression would appear similar to the following:

ID	FirstName	LastName	Manager
18	Greg	Oltman	
9	Robert	Jones	Amanda Smith
10	Tonya	Green	Amanda Smith
11	Michael	McDonald	Amanda Smith
12	Leon	DeLuca	Michael Kidwell
13	John	Michaels	Michael Kidwell
14	Susan	Palmer	Michael Kidwell
16	Jennifer	Jones	Michael Kidwell
17	Tyrone	Baseman	Michael Kidwell
8	Amanda	Smith	Greg Oltman
15	Michael	Kidwell	Greg Oltman
19	Cindy	Regal	Greg Oltman
21	John	Ramsey	Greg Oltman

Theta Joins

Whereas equi-, left- and right-joins are designed to find equivalences between records in related tables, a Theta join is used to return records that have differences between fields in two tables. Each of the two fields in question must be of the same data type. It is not possible to directly create a theta join in the **Query Design View**. Rather, the join is specified by adding the *Not* operator, <>, along with a field reference in one of the criteria cells.

As an example, take two tables, one of which stores employee information, including *StartDate*. The second table stores human resource information, including an *HR StartDate* field. Let's assume that under ideal conditions, the date fields in both tables should be the same. If you were interesting in mining those records between the two tables where a difference in start date occurs, you would use a theta join.

A query to model a theta join based on this example would appear similar to the following in **Query Design View**.

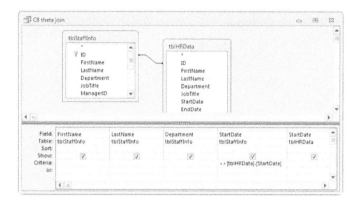

The key to the theta join is the criteria expression, **<>[tblHRData].[Startdate]** in the *StartDate* field of the tblStaffInfo table. Note that the two tables are joined on a common field, *EmployeeID*. This is required of a theta join or the query would not be able to find the appropriate *HR Response Date* for comparison against the employee *StartDate*.

Running a query such as the one illustrated above would produce results similar to the following in **Datasheet View**.

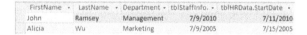

Asking Multiple AND Questions in a Single Field

There are times when you want to ask an **And** question against a single field. For example, in a database that stores employee skills in a one-to-many relationship to employees, a question of this type may be expressed as *Who has management **and** facilitation skills?*

You might think that this question can simply be expressed using the following criteria expression:

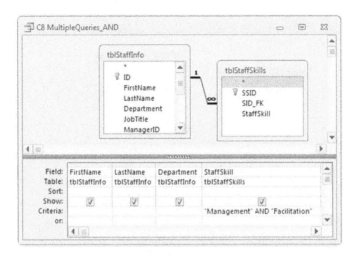

This query will always yield an empty record set. The reason is that there is never a situation where both skills are stored in the same field and all queries resolve criteria expressions one record at a time, and even if they were stored in a single field the syntax above would be incorrect as you'd really need to search on *management* and *facilitation* as if they were fragments in the single field.

SQL is an interesting and powerful language and often there are two or more approaches to yield the desired results. In this case we can illustrate at least 3 different approaches. In two of the cases we'll need as many copies of the skills table (or as many copies of a separate query) as the number of criteria we are AND'ing together. The third approach is simpler and would work well if the number of criteria exceeds 3 or so.

The first solution is to use two copies of the table containing the field your *AND* question is focused on. When you add a second copy of the table, you may need to manually draw the appropriate join line from the table representing the *one* side of the *one-to-many* join. The field of interest, *Skill*, is represented twice, once from the original table and a second time from a copy of the table. Each part of the *AND* question is treated as a separate criteria in the *Skill* field. Such a query would appear similar to the following in design view:

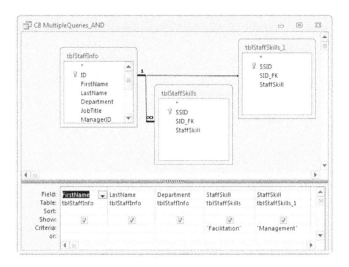

Running such a query would yield results similar to these:

FirstName	LastName	Department	tblStaffSkills.StaffSkill	tblStaffSkills_1.StaffSkill
Tonya	Green	Finance	Facilitation	Management
Michael	Kidwell	IT	Facilitation	Management

In such a design, searching on a third skill would involve adding a third copy of tblStaffSkills and creating a third criteria in a separate column. This approach becomes burdensome as the number of criteria AND'ed together increases.

The second approach is conceptually similar to the first example but uses separate queries in order to ask the individual criteria questions. So in the illustration below, qry1 asks which staff have management as a listed skill and qry2 asks the same question but for facilitation skill. The two queries are joined on the StaffID field. The results of running this query are identical to that illustrated above.

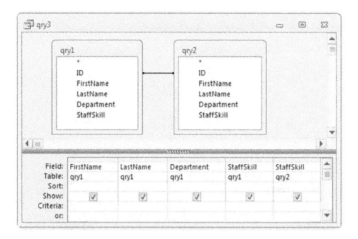

Like the first example, if you choose to add a third skill in the search you need to first create a third query which asks for that specific skill, then join that query to one of the other queries. The total number of queries you must create using this approach is *n+1* where *n* is the number of individual criteria. The additional query serves as the master container to pull the individual criteria queries together. Like the first approach, this method becomes less useful as the number of individual criteria increase.

The final approach is more elegant in that you work with single query and a minimum number of tables. The query at first appears similar to the initial, incorrect approach illustrated on Page 73. Closer inspection however indicates that this is a totals query (note the **Total** row as illustrated below).

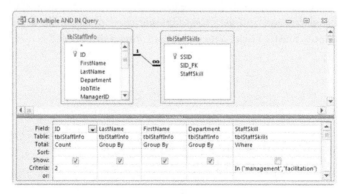

There are two components to this approach. The first is to use the **In()** function to list the two or more criteria you wish to search for. Because this is a totals query you must set the **Total** parameter to *Where* in order for the criteria search to be applied. The second component is to count on a unique field – in the example above it's the employee *ID* field. The criteria is set to *2*, which in this example maps directly to the number of terms in the **In()** function.

This query will also yield the same results as the previous two queries. The way it's different however is in the fact that, because it is a totals query, it groups on LastName and the other, non-criteria fields (as indicated by the **Group By** setting) and returns up to two rows – in those cases mapping to the staff that have both management and facilitation skills. Because we only want to see those staff that appear twice in the results, the Count criteria for the *ID* field is set to *2*. This has the interesting effect of filtering the results. If staff *ID* only appear once prior to applying the count criteria of 2 they do not appear in the final results, while staff whose *ID* count does equal two – meaning they have both the requested skills appear in the final results.

Such an approach is more elegant when the number of search terms increases. To search on 4 skills, you would first list them in the **In()** function and then set the *ID* **Count** criteria to *4*.

SQL Statements and Special Joins

The essence of the self join involves referencing a second copy of a table. SQL handles this by allowing you to create an alias name for the second copy of the table., although Access handles this alias creation differently than other database management systems.

SQL Statement	Description
SELECT tblStaffInfo.ID, tblStaffInfo.FirstName, tblStaffInfo.LastName, tblStaffInfo_1.FirstName, tblStaffInfo_1.LastName FROM tblStaffInfo LEFT JOIN tblStaffInfo AS tblStaffInfo_1 ON tblStaffInfo.ManagerID = tblStaffInfo_1.ID;	This statement lists managers of staff using a self join. Because managers are themselves staff, their StaffID appears in the ManagerID field for each of their managed staff. The LEFT JOIN ensures that managers are also listed in the results. Note the second copy of *tblStaffInfo* referred to in several locations as *tblStaffInfo_1*
SELECT tblStaffInfo.FirstName, tblStaffInfo.LastName, tblStaffInfo.Department, tblStaffInfo.StartDate FROM tblStaffInfo INNER JOIN tblHRData ON tblStaffInfo.ID = tblHRData.ID WHERE ((((tblStaffInfo.StartDate)<>[tblHRData].[StartDate]));	A theta join is implemented as a negation criteria (not equal to) against two fields of the same data type. Here the example is looking for records, with the same StaffID (hence the join) where the start date in the tblStaffInfo table isn't equal to the start date in the tblHRData.
SELECT Count(tblStaffInfo.ID) AS CountOfID, tblStaffInfo.LastName, tblStaffInfo.FirstName, tblStaffInfo.Department FROM tblStaffInfo INNER JOIN tblStaffSkills ON tblStaffInfo.ID = tblStaffSkills.SID_FK WHERE (((tblStaffSkills.StaffSkill) In ("management","facilitation"))) GROUP BY tblStaffInfo.LastName, tblStaffInfo.FirstName, tblStaffInfo.Department HAVING (((Count(tblStaffInfo.ID))=2));	This is the SQL statement behind the last example of how to ask multiple questions against a single field. As discussed the query becomes a totals query and counts against a unique field (here the staffID from tblStaffInfo. The criteria, associated with the WHERE clause pulls records that match either *management* or *facilitation*. The final selection element, after the HAVING clause, only displays those records where the county of StaffID is 2 - indicating a staff that had two matches to the requested skill.

Chapter 9 | Crosstab Queries and PivotTables

Select queries are powerful tools for asking questions of your database data. We previously discussed Totals Queries – a subset of a select query – that adds additional functionality to group data and provide summary functions to numeric data within each group. Crosstab and PivotTables are related to Totals Queries but include the concept of a *dimension*. In a totals query you can think of a field you group by as being a single dimension. The difference between totals queries and crosstab or PivotTables is that the latter provide you with the ability to summarize against two or more dimensions, and in the case of PivotTables, to include sub and grand totals. PivotTables, as their name suggests, also allow for real-time reordering of dimensions, making the discovery of patterns in your data an easy task. PivotTables are such sophisticated data analysis tools that they fall into the realm of OLAP (on-line analytical processing) data mining.

Overview of Crosstab Queries

A crosstab query calculates a sum, average, or other aggregate function on one field and groups the results against two or more related fields. This produces a worksheet-like display where the summary values are contained within cells in the grid and the grouped fields make up the row and column headers.

Crosstab queries are closely related to totals queries. The following example illustrates the relationship.

Consider a totals query that sums the total project budget for each project by department. The query as constructed would appear as:

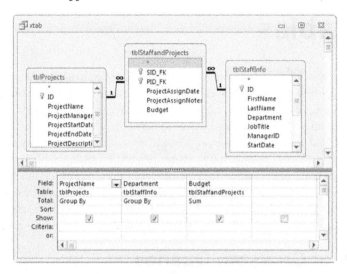

And the result of such a query would appear similar to the following:

ProjectName	Department	SumOfBudget
Cloud Storage Implementation	Finance	$7,500.00
Cloud Storage Implementation	IT	$55,000.00
Cloud Storage Implementation	Marketing	$7,500.00
Financial System Reengineering	Finance	$97,000.00
Financial System Reengineering	IT	$15,000.00
Marketing Survey	Finance	$2,500.00
Marketing Survey	Marketing	$62,500.00
Server upgrade	Finance	$500.00
Server upgrade	IT	$50,500.00
Server upgrade	Management	$500.00
Six Sigma Implementation	Finance	$15,000.00
Six Sigma Implementation	IT	$22,500.00
Six Sigma Implementation	Management	$15,000.00
Six Sigma Implementation	Marketing	$15,000.00
VOIP migration	Finance	$10,000.00

Comparison between departments for total project budget is difficult because of the repeating nature of the department field values (once for each different project).

The same data, presented in a crosstab query, would appear similar to the following:

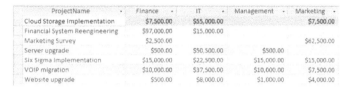

ProjectName	Finance	IT	Management	Marketing
Cloud Storage Implementation	$7,500.00	$55,000.00		$7,500.00
Financial System Reengineering	$97,000.00	$15,000.00		
Marketing Survey	$2,500.00			$62,500.00
Server upgrade	$500.00	$50,500.00	$500.00	
Six Sigma Implementation	$15,000.00	$22,500.00	$15,000.00	$15,000.00
VOIP migration	$10,000.00	$37,500.00	$10,000.00	$7,500.00
Website upgrade	$500.00	$8,000.00	$1,000.00	$4,000.00

This view should strike you as different. The column headings that have appeared in every query up to this point are gone and have been replaced by field values – in this case the specific names of departments. Unlike the previous query it's easy to see what the total budget by project and department is. A crosstab query summarizes numeric data (usually using a SUM or COUNT function) and plots the results against a minimum of two fields, denoted by the properties *Row heading* and *Column heading*. Unlike a regular select query, whichever field is denoted as the *column heading* uses field values instead of the name of the field. A crosstab query may group on up to three fields as the *Row heading* values.

The name *crosstab* is derived from shortening the term *Cross Tabulation*. This term is not standard in other relational database management systems.

Creating a Crosstab Query Using a Wizard

The **Crosstab Query Wizard** is limited in that it only works from data in a single table or query. If you need to pull data from two or more tables, first build a select query based on those tables, and then use the query as the data source for your crosstab query. In the following example the crosstab query sums staff budget by project and department.

How to Create a Crosstab Query Using the Wizard

Step 1.   From the **Create** ribbon, in the **Queries** group, choose **Query** Wizard.

Step 2.   In the **New Query** dialog box, choose **Crosstab Query Wizard** and choose **OK**. The first dialog box of the **Crosstab Query Wizard** will appear similar to the following:

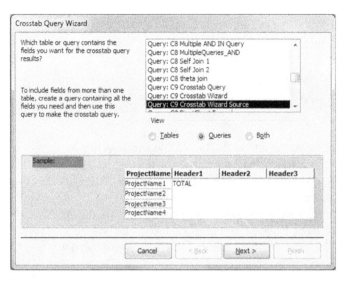

Step 3.   Select the table or query that will supply the data. If desired, use the **View** area to control which type of record source is displayed. Choose **Next**. The second dialog box of the **Crosstab Query Wizard** will appear similar to the following:

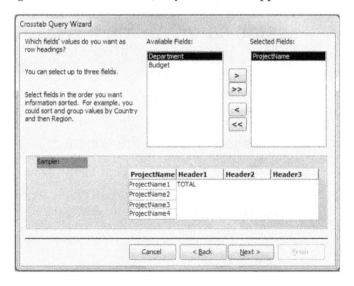

Step 4.   Add the field or fields you wish to use as row headings (you can choose up to 3). Note that the field or fields you choose will be used to group crosstab data. Choose **Next**. The third dialog box of the **Crosstab Query Wizard** will appear similar to the following:

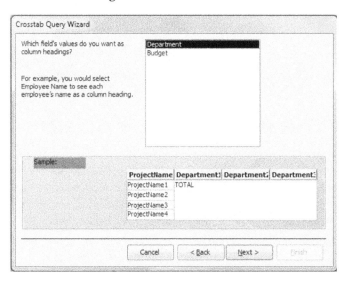

Step 5.   Select the field that will serve as the column headings. Note that this is the other field that will serve to group the crosstab data. Choose **Next**. The fourth dialog box of the **Crosstab Query Wizard** will appear similar to the following:

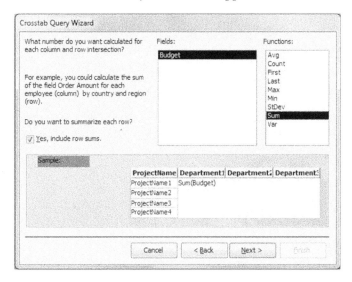

Step 6.   Choose the field that will supply the summary data from the **Fields** list, then choose the function to apply from the **Functions** list. Choose **Next**.

Step 7.   Type a name for the crosstab query, then choose **Finish**. If you chose to view the query the results will appear similar to the following:

ProjectName	Total Of Bud	Finance	IT	Managemer	Marketing
Cloud Storage Implementation	$70,000.00	$7,500.00	$55,000.00		$7,500.00
Financial System Reengineering	$112,000.00	$97,000.00	$15,000.00		
Marketing Survey	$65,000.00	$2,500.00			$62,500.00
Server upgrade	$51,500.00	$500.00	$50,500.00	$500.00	
Six Sigma Implementation	$67,500.00	$15,000.00	$22,500.00	$15,000.00	$15,000.00
VOIP migration	$65,000.00	$10,000.00	$37,500.00	$10,000.00	$7,500.00
Website upgrade	$13,500.00	$500.00	$8,000.00	$1,000.00	$4,000.00

Creating a Crosstab Query from Scratch

If you create a crosstab query on your own, you need to identify the field or fields that will serve as row headings, the field that will serve as the column heading, and the field that will supply the summary data. A crosstab query appears similar to any other query when viewed in **Query Design View**. The major distinction is the presence of an additional row in the **Field Grid** named *Crosstab*. You use this row to specify crosstab-specific parameters.

One advantage to creating a crosstab query from scratch is that you do not need to create a multiple-table query ahead of time when working with two or more tables.

How to Create a Crosstab Query from Scratch

Step 1.   From the **Create** tab, in the **Queries** group, select **Query Design**.

Step 2.   Using the **Show Tables** dialog box, add the table or tables for the crosstab query. When finished, close the dialog by choosing **Close**.

Step 3.   From the **Query Type** group, choose **Crosstab**.

Step 4.   To the **Field Grid**, add the fields that will serve as the **row** and **column headings**, as well as the summary values.

Step 5.   For each field column in the **Field Grid**, select the appropriate crosstab query option from the drop-down list in the **Crosstab** cell.

Option	Description
Row Heading	The field will supply values to be used as row headings. You can select up to three fields to serve as row headings.
Column Heading	The field will supply values to be used as column headings. Only one field may be indicated as the column heading.
Value	Values from this field are summarized using one of the aggregate functions. In addition to setting the **Value** option, this field must also have an aggregate function selected from the **Total** cell.
(Not shown)	Any field with the **(Not shown)** option may be used to supply criteria to filter the resulting records.

Step 6. For the field with the **Crosstab** option set to **Value**, select the appropriate aggregate function from the **Total** cell.

Step 7. If you wish to include a column that totals the entries for each row, use the following procedure: Add a second copy of the field used to supply the **Value** for the crosstab query. Set its **Crosstab** option to **Row Heading** and the **Total** option to the appropriate function (usually **Sum** or **Count**).

Step 8. If you wish to add a criteria to the crosstab query, use the following procedure: Add the desired field (it can be a duplicate of a field already on the **Field Grid**) to the **Field Grid**. In the **Total** cell, choose the **Expression** option. In the **Criteria** cell, type in your criteria expression. Repeat this procedure for any additional fields and/or criteria expressions.

Step 9. Run the query by changing to **Datasheet View**.

Step 10. If desired, save the query design.

How to Control Column Heading Order

In a crosstab query, column order is determined by applying an ascending order sort. For example, if the column values in a crosstab query consist of the month name from a date field, the dates would appear in the order *April, August, December,* etc. You can adjust the order in which column headings in a crosstab query appear by modifying the **Column Headings** property. By doing so you specify the actual field values in the order in which you wish them to appear.

Step 1. Open an existing crosstab query in **Query Design View**, or create a new crosstab query.

Step 2. Select the query by clicking anywhere in the **Table Area**, away from a table or query object.

Step 3. From the **Query Design** toolbar, select the **Properties** button.

Step 4.   In the **Column Headings** text box, type the column heading values in the desired order. For text values, contain each field value in quotes and separate field values with a comma.

Step 5.   Run the crosstab query and check that the column headings appear in the desired order.

Column heading values must exactly match those of the field values. They must be enclosed in double-quotes and be separated from one another by commas. An example of a string to order month names chronologically would appear as: "January", "February", "March", "April", etc. The values you enter for **Column Headings** must exactly match the field values stored in the table or query.

PivotTables and PivotCharts

A PivotTable is an interactive data analysis tool that is capable of summarizing large data sets. You can think of a crosstab query as being a very simple PivotTable. The difference is that the crosstab is limited to at most 4 summary fields (3 row headings and 1 column heading) and can only summarize against one field. PivotTables lack these limitations and in addition, add powerful grouping functions and include the ability to drag summary fields between the row and column areas. This ability to instantly reorganize summary data gives the PivotTable its name. A PivotChart is like a PivotTable but provides a graphical summary of the data. PivotTables and PivotCharts are simply views of tables or queries. If the **Allow PivotTable View** or **Allow PivotChart View** properties are set for a form, PivotTables and PivotCharts may be generated from a form view as well.

The most useful aspect of PivotTables is the ability to quickly reorder the level of grouping. This permits you to look for trends within the data which may not be as apparent when viewing the individual records in the database. You reorder a PivotTable or PivotChart by dragging the field or fields used to group the information to reflect a new grouping order or arrangement. PivotTables and PivotCharts as implemented in Microsoft Access are similar to those available in Microsoft Excel.

A major difference between PivotTables and Crosstab queries is that the former may not be used as a data source for a report while the latter may. If you need to create a report from an existing PivotTable, export the PivotTable to Microsoft Excel and use Excel's built in PivotTable report templates. See the discussion of PivotTable toolbar commands on page 90 for the Export to Excel command.

As an example, consider the partial results from a query such as that illustrated below. The query pulls data about projects, the department associated with each assigned staff, and the budget for each staff member.

ProjectName	Budget	Department	StartDate
VOIP migration	$10,000.00	Finance	10/1/2014
Financial System Reengineering	$95,000.00	Finance	10/1/2013
Six Sigma Implementation	$15,000.00	Finance	1/2/2012
Server upgrade	$500.00	Finance	9/15/2014
Financial System Reengineering	$1,000.00	Finance	10/1/2013
Marketing Survey	$2,500.00	Finance	6/1/2013
Website upgrade	$500.00	Finance	10/1/2011
Financial System Reengineering	$1,000.00	Finance	10/1/2013
Cloud Storage Implementation	$7,500.00	Finance	2/1/2014
VOIP migration	$7,500.00	IT	10/1/2014
Financial System Reengineering	$7,500.00	IT	10/1/2013
Website upgrade	$4,000.00	IT	10/1/2011
Six Sigma Implementation	$7,500.00	IT	1/2/2012
Server upgrade	$7,500.00	IT	9/15/2014
Website upgrade	$4,000.00	IT	10/1/2011

In one of many configurations possible in a PivotTable, the following example sums budgets by project, department, and by year. The Year field has been configured to create subtotals while the budget data has been configured to create grand totals. These are features not available to crosstab queries.

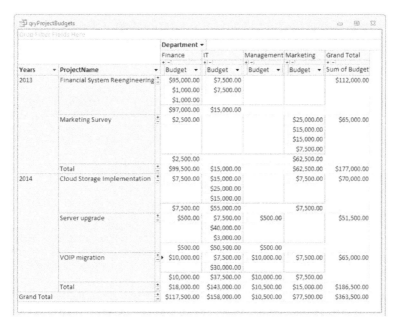

Components of a PivotTable

PivotTables consist of four field areas: row, column, detail, and filter. The row and column areas are where you place fields you wish to use as grouping levels and the detail area consists of the fields you wish to summarize. The detail field must be of a data type which permits summarization (such as number or currency fields), or it must consist of unique records (such as the table's *primary key* field) in order to count records. Non-unique fields and field types such as memo cannot be used for detail fields. The Filter field area is used to supply any additional overall filtering you may desire.

At a minimum, you design a PivotTable with one field for grouping (located either in the Row or Column area) and a field you wish to summarize (located in the detail area). You may add multiple fields to any region of the PivotTable. For example, placing two fields such as **Department** and **Section** in the Row Field area will create grouping first based on **Department** and then within departments, by **Section**.

The following illustration highlights the main components of a PivotTable.

Filter Field   Column Field

		Finance	IT	Management	Marketing	Grand Total
StartDate ▼	ProjectName ▼	Sum of Budget	Sum of Budget	Sum of Budget	Sum of Budget	Sum of Budget
10/1/2011	Website upgrade	$500.00	$8,000.00	$1,000.00	$4,000.00	$13,500.00
	Total	$500.00	$8,000.00	$1,000.00	$4,000.00	$13,500.00
1/2/2012	Six Sigma Implementation	$15,000.00	$22,500.00	$15,000.00	$15,000.00	$67,500.00
	Total	$15,000.00	$22,500.00	$15,000.00	$15,000.00	$67,500.00
2/1/2014	Cloud Storage Implementation	$7,500.00	$55,000.00		$7,500.00	$70,000.00
	Total	$7,500.00	$55,000.00		$7,500.00	$70,000.00
6/1/2014	Marketing Survey	$2,500.00			$62,500.00	$65,000.00
	Total	$2,500.00			$62,500.00	$65,000.00
9/15/2014	Server upgrade	$500.00	$50,500.00	$500.00		$51,500.00
	Total	$500.00	$50,500.00	$500.00		$51,500.00
10/1/2014	Financial System Reengineering	$97,000.00	$15,000.00			$112,000.00
	VOIP migration	$10,000.00	$37,500.00	$10,000.00	$7,500.00	$65,000.00
	Total	$107,000.00	$52,500.00	$10,000.00	$7,500.00	$177,000.00
Grand Total		$133,000.00	$188,500.00	$26,500.00	$96,500.00	$444,500.00

Row Field   Detail Field

Component	Description
Filter Field	Optional area used to apply filtering to the entire PivotTable. Any field or fields dragged into this area become active filters, although the default *All* will be automatically applied. You use the drop down arrow associated with the filter field to further narrow your choices.
Column Field	A field area which groups data and arranges the grouping by columns across the top of the PivotTable. More than one field may be used in this area.
Row Field	A field area which groups data and arranges the grouping by rows along the left edge of the PivotTable. More than one field may be used in this area.
Detail Field	Contains the field or fields which are being summarized. In addition to standard arithmetic summaries such as Sum, Count or Average, you may also create *calculated totals* in this area.

Creating a PivotTable

You create a PivotTable by working with an existing table or query, or with a form bound to a table or query. When you create a PivotTable, the design is saved with the underlying table or query. The mechanics of creating and manipulating PivotTables is the same regardless of the underlying data source.

How to Create a PivotTable

Step 1.   Open the desired table or query in **Datasheet** view, or open the desired data bound form in **Form** view.

Step 2.   From the **View** group on the **Home** ribbon, choose **PivotTable View.** A window similar to the following will appear:

In addition to the PivotTable design window illustrated above, a list of fields from the underlying table or query will appear in the **Field list**. This window appears similar to the following:

Step 3.   Drag the desired fields from the **Field List** to one of the specific areas marked on the **PivotTable** window. The areas of the **PivotTable** are discussed beginning on page 88.

Step 4.   If desired, modify various properties of the PivotTable or of individual fields using the **PivotTable** ribbon.

PivotTable Ribbon

Group	Description
View	Switches between Datasheet, PivotTable ,PivotChart, SQL, and design views.
Show/Hide	Controls the visibility of various components of the PivotTable, the Field List, and/or data details.
Selections	Permits the creation and removal of custom groups using data in the row or column fields.
Filter & Sort	Sets sort ordering and the display of top *n* or bottom *n* values.
Data	Refresh data or export PivotTable data to Microsoft Excel.
Active Field	Expand, collapse, remove or move the current field.
Tools	Manage field properties and/or establish predefined or custom calculations for the detail data.

If a table or query contains fields of the Date/Time data type, those fields will appear in the **Field List** with grouping options (such as *By Week* or *By Month*) automatically applied.

How to Add Fields to a PivotTable

Once the initial PivotTable window has been opened, you are ready to add fields to the desired PivotTable areas.

Step 1.   If the **Field List** is not visible, open it by choosing the **Field List** command from the **Show/Hide** group.

Step 2.   Drag the desired field from the **Field List** to the appropriate area of the PivotTable. Use the discussion beginning on page 88 as a guide if desired.

If you wish to create nested levels within a row or column, drag the next field to the right or left of the current row or column field.

How to Remove a Field from a PivotTable

Step 1.   Select the desired field within the row, column or detail area. The selected field name will appear in Bold once selected.

Step 2.   Right-click on the field and from the shortcut menu, choose **Remove**, or, choose **Remove Field** from the **Active Field** group, or press the *Delete* key.

How to Apply a Summary Function

Step 1.   Select the desired field from the **Detail** area.

Step 2.   From the **Tools** group, choose **AutoCalc**.

Step 3.   Choose the desired summary function from the drop down list.

Summary fields are treated like regular fields in a PivotTable and may be deleted or dragged to another position within the detail area. You may not drag a summary field into any of the other PivotTable areas.

How to Create Sub and Grand Totals

In many cases, applying a summary function automatically creates the appropriate sub and grand totals, although you may need to apply the appropriate summary function to data in the detail area prior to establishing sub and/or grand totals. A subtotal will only be applied to a field in the row or column area if the field contains grouped data that support summary functions.

Step 1.   If a summary function has not be applied to the detail area, begin by selecting the appropriate field in the detail area and then choose **Autocalc** from the **Tools** group. Most totals involve applying the **Sum** function.

Step 2.   To establish grand or sub totals, select the desired row or column field.

Step 3.   From the **Tools** group, select **Subtotal**.

 Grand totals appear to the right and bottom of the PivotTable. If you wish to move column grand totals to the left, from the **Properties** window for the PivotTable, select the **Behavior** tab and choose **Display Right to Left**.

How to Reorder a Grouped Field

The power of PivotTables is the ability to quickly reorganize its structure. By moving row or column fields - either to the right or left of other fields, or by moving between row and column areas - you can create a reorganized view of your summary data. Such ability to reorganize may assist in your analysis of the summary data.

You drag fields within or between the column and row field areas to create new grouping orders. As you drag a field, a blue insertion bar indicates where the field will be placed when you release the left mouse button.

Step 1.   Position the mouse pointer over the desired field name and hold down the left mouse button.

Step 2.   Drag the mouse to the new location and release the mouse button. As you drag the field a blue bar will follow and indicate the current drop location. Continue moving the field until you reach the desired target.

Step 3.   Release the left mouse button.

 The **Undo** command does not work when you move fields around within a PivotTable. If you make a mistake, drag the field again, either to the desired location or to its former location.

How to Save a PivotTable Design

PivotTables are saved as part of the structure of the underlying table, query, or form. You may only have one PivotTable design per table, query, or form. If you create or modify a PivotTable and do not choose to save the design, your changes are not stored.

Step 1.   From the **Quick Access** toolbar, choose **Save**.

If you create or modify a PivotTable and attempt to close the table or query datasheet or close the form, you will be asked if you wish to save the design changes. Choosing *Yes* is the same action as electing to save the PivotTable design.

How to View an Existing PivotTable

There is no direct way to open a table, query or form and view its underlying PivotTable.

Step 1.   Open the desired table, query or form.

Step 2.   From the **View** group, choose **PivotTable View**.

How to Clear a PivotTable Design

There is no direct method of removing a PivotTable design from a table or query. You must manually remove all of the fields on the PivotTable.

Step 1.   Open the PivotTable.

Step 2.   Select a field on the PivotTable.

Step 3.   Right-click on the field and from the shortcut menu, choose **Remove**, or, press the *Delete* key.

Step 4.   Continue steps 2 and 3 until all of the fields have been removed.

If your PivotTable included summary fields, open the **Field List** and remove them as well. Select each summary field (they will be arranged under the heading **Totals**) and right-click. From the shortcut menu, choose **Delete**.

Creating a PivotChart

PivotCharts are similar to PivotTables in that they may be based on an existing table, query, or form. You generate a PivotChart by choosing **PivotChart** from the **View** group when a table or query is open, although for forms you must first enable the **Allow PivotChart View** property associated with the form.

The major difference between PivotCharts and PivotTables is in the display of the detail data. PivotCharts by default switch to a summary or count view of detail data whereas detail data may easily be examined in a PivotTable. Also, PivotCharts use *category* and *series* areas rather than row and column areas.

A series is a group of related data points. For example, project budgets for a department over time represents a series. Typically there are two or more related sets of data in a series. In a large organization, each department would be an element within the greater series. Series constitute the data that appears in the body of the graph and are associated with the graph's legend.

A category maps to the data presented along the chart's X-axis. In the example of project funding by department, if departments constitute the series then projects would occupy the category field.

Usually category and series fields can be interchanged, and hence the pivot component. The requirement is that the two or more subjects are related by some field that can be counted or summed. Since you can consider funding by project and then department, or by department and then project, the two fields may occupy either the category or series fields while the funding amount is the entity which, in this case, can be summarized by totaling.

Filter Field

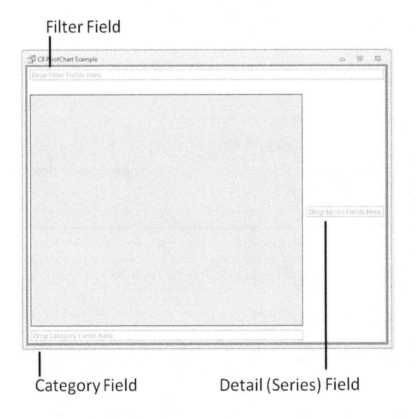

Category Field   Detail (Series) Field

Component	Description
Filter Field	Optional area used to apply filtering to the entire PivotTable. Any field or fields dragged into this area become active filters, although the default *All* will be automatically applied. You use the drop down arrow associated with the filter field to further narrow your choices.
Category Field	A field area which groups data and arranges the grouping by columns across the top of the PivotTable. More than one field may be used in this area.
Series Field	Contains the field or fields which are being summarized. In addition to standard arithmetic summaries such as Sum, Count or Average, you may also create *calculated totals* in this area.

How to Create a PivotChart

Step 1.   Open the desired table or query in **Datasheet** view, or open the desired data bound form in **Form** view.

Step 2.   From the **View** group on the **Home** ribbon, choose **PivotChart View.** A window similar to the following will appear:

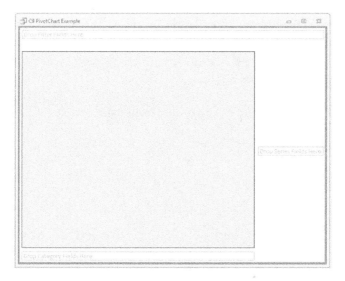

In addition to the PivotChart design window illustrated above, a list of fields from the underlying table or query will appear in the **Field list**. This window appears similar to the following:

Step 3.   Drag the desired fields from the **Field List** to one of the specific areas marked on the **PivotChart** window. The areas of the **PivotChart** are discussed beginning on page 95.

Step 4.   If desired, modify various properties of the PivotChart or of individual fields using the **PivotChart** ribbon.

PivotChart Ribbon

Group	Description
View	Switches between Datasheet, PivotTable ,PivotChart , SQL, and design views.
Show/Hide	Controls the visibility of various components of the PivotChart (such as data legends and the drop zones), the Field List, and/or data details.
Filter & Sort	Sets sort ordering and the display of top *n* or bottom *n* values.
Data	Refresh data or export PivotTable data to Microsoft Excel.
Active Field	Expand, collapse, remove or move the current field, or switch a field between row and column on the chart.
Type	Choose a chart type from a predefined set of types.
Tools	Manage field or chart properties and/or establish predefined or custom calculations for the detail data.

How to Add Fields to a PivotChart

Once the initial PivotChart window has been opened, you are ready to add fields to the desired PivotChart areas. As previously discussed you should consider whether a field is best suited to serve as a *category*, *series* or summary field.

Step 1.   If the **Field List** is not visible, open it by choosing the **Field List** command from the **Show/Hide** group.

Step 2.   Drag the desired field from the **Field List** to the appropriate area of the PivotChart. Use the discussion beginning on page 88 as a guide if desired.

How to Remove a Field from a PivotChart

Step 1.   Select the desired field within the row, column or detail area. The selected field name will appear in bold once selected.

Step 2.   Right-click on the field and from the shortcut menu, choose **Remove**, or, choose **Remove Field** from the **Active Field** group, or press the *Delete* key.

How to Apply a Summary Function

Step 1.   Select the desired field from the **Detail** area. For a PivotChart this is usually a button in the upper left corner of the chart area with the name of the function currently applied and the field name.

Step 2.   From the **Tools** group, choose **AutoCalc**.

Step 3.   Choose the desired summary function from the drop down list.

How to Change the Chart Type

Once you have the basic arrangement of category, series, and summary data laid out you can change the chart type to best suit your needs.

Step 1.   If the **Chart Type** button in the **Type** group is not enabled, activate it by clicking on the chart area. The chart **Properties** dialog will appear similar to the following:

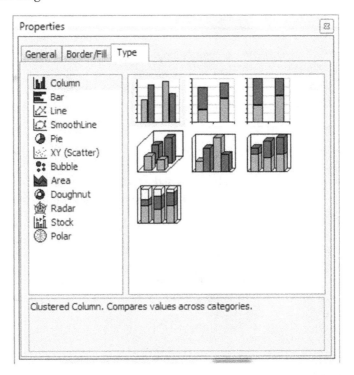

Step 2.   Use the area to the left of the **Type** tab to select a general category, then select a specific chart type from the options in the right-hand pane. As you choose a particular style the underlying PivotChart will change.

Step 3.   Close the **Properties** dialog box when done.

How to Clear a PivotChart Design

There is no direct method of removing a PivotChart design from a table or query. You must manually remove all of the fields on the PivotChart.

Step 1.   Open the PivotChart.

Step 2.   Select a field on the PivotChart.

Step 3.   Press the *Delete* key or drag the field to the **Field List**.

Step 4.   Continue steps 2 and 3 until all of the fields have been removed.

SQL, Crosstab, and PivotTables

The SQL Language lacks any crosstab or PivotTable syntax. These structures tend to specialize in data analysis and that goes beyond the original SQL language specification. That said, there are numerous articles, both in print and available on-line, that provide workarounds for creating crosstab-like query results using SQL. These approaches are cleaver implementations of complex SQL statements but are beyond the scope of this book.

PivotTables (and PivotCharts) are terms specifically trademarked by Microsoft Corporation. Other vendors provide analysis tools with similar functionality and the general term used is *pivot table*.

Chapter 10 | Action Queries

All of the queries discussed to this point are essentially *Select* queries and their common thread has been the selection of data from one or more tables. *Action* queries perform actions against an existing table to update, delete or append data, or in the case of a make table query, to create a new table in the database. They are similar to select queries in that they can accept criteria and work against a subset of table data. In this way it is helpful to think of action queries as being utility or maintenance functions whereas select queries are used for analysis. An important difference between a select and an action query is in the way the action query is run. Opening an action query in **Datasheet View** simply shows the records that will be acted on if the action query is run. To run the action query, you use the **Run** command.

The **Run** command may also be used to run a select query. It is not a good idea to routinely use this command as it is easier to inadvertently run an action query without thinking of the ramifications. Once run, the effect of an action query may not be undone. Thus, it is highly recommended that you train yourself to use the **Datasheet View** command to run select queries and to inspect the potential effects of an action query, and to reserve the **Run** command exclusively for running an action query.

Make Table Query

A make table query creates a new table in an Access database and uses fields from existing tables or queries as both the source of field names and data types, and field values. Specific field properties such as **input masks** and **primary keys** are not included when the table is created.

Points on Make Table Queries

- You can create a table in any Access database, not just the current database.

- If you wish to combine fields from two or more tables, add those tables to the **Table Area** and select the desired fields.

- You can write field expressions to create newly named fields that combine field values from two or more fields, or use operators or functions to generate the field values.

- If you elect to use the name of an existing table, the make table query will delete the existing table before creating a new one. You will be prompted before this action takes effect.

How to Create a Make Table Query

Step 1.   From the **Create** ribbon, in the **Queries** group, choose **Query Design.**

Step 2.   Using the **Show Tables** dialog box, add the table(s) and/or queries that will supply the field values. When finished, close the dialog by choosing **Close.**

Step 3.   From the **Query Tools** ribbon in the **Query Type** group, select **Make-Table Query**. A dialog box similar to the following will appear:

Option	Description
Table Name	Enter a name for the new table or choose an existing table name from the drop-down list. Note that if you choose an existing table, it will be deleted before the query creates a new table.
Current Database	Select if you wish to create the table in the current database. This is the default setting.
Another Database	Select if you wish to create the table in another Access database. You must supply a full drive, path, and file name specification.
File Name	When creating a table in another database, type the full drive, path, and file name of the target database.

Step 4.   Type or select a unique table name, or if creating a table in another Access database, select **Another Database** and type a valid database drive, path, and file name in the **File Name** text box. Choose **OK** when done.

Step 5.   Add the desired fields from table or query objects in the **Table Area**.

Step 6.   If desired, establish new fields by combining two or more existing fields using a field expression. Refer to page 37 for details, or, establish new fields by creating function expressions.

Step 7.   If you wish to limit the records placed in the new table, create criteria expressions in the appropriate field columns. Refer to page 21 for details.

Step 8.   To view the records that will make up the new table, select the **View** button from the **Results** group or, to run the query, select the **Run** button from the **Results** group.

The following table outlines the query properties that are significant to a make table query, especially if you are creating a table in another database. Refer to page 14 for discussion of common query properties.

Important Make Table Query Properties

Property	Description
Source Database	Provides the name of the database that is supplying the fields and field values for the new table. Generally this value is *(current)*.
Source Connect Str	Sets a connection string to the source database, if required. If the source database is password protected, the password would be specified here.
Destination Table	Specifies the name of the destination table. This is the table name you selected in Step 4 above.
Destination DB	Specifies the name of the destination database. This would be the value you typed into the File Name box in Step 4 above.
Destination Connect Str	Sets a connection string to the destination database, if required. If the destination database is password protected, the password would be specified here.
Use Transaction	Controls whether Access uses *Transactions* when processing an action query. Transactions ensure that if the query fails, the records are restored to their original state. The default is *No*. Only set to *Yes* if your query is creating a table in another database and you require the ability to roll back changes if a communication error occurs.

Append Query

Append queries add records to an existing table. The table can be any table in an Access database. When you create an append query, a new row, **Append**, appears in the **Field Grid**. This row is used to match the query fields with the fields in the destination table.

Points on Append Queries

- When you append records to a table, any validation rules, input masks, required fields, and primary key constraints present in the destination table must be honored. Records that fail any of these constraints are not appended.

- You need not append records with the same number of fields as the destination table (unless the missing fields map to required fields in the destination table - this would include primary key fields as these may never be empty or null).

- Field names need not match between the append query and the destination table, but field data types must match.

How to Create an Append Query

Step 1.   From the **Create** ribbon, in the **Queries** group, choose **Query Design.**

Step 2.   Using the **Show Tables** dialog box, add the table(s) and/or queries that will supply the field values. When finished, close the dialog by choosing **Close**.

Step 3.   From the **Query Tools** ribbon in the **Query Type** group, select **Append Query**. A dialog box similar to the following will appear:

Option	Description
Table Name	Choose an existing table name from the drop-down list.
Current Database	Select if you wish to append to a table in the current database. This is the default setting.
Another Database	Select if you wish to append to a table in another Access database. You must supply a full drive, path, and file name specification.
File Name	When appending to a table in another database, type the full drive, path, and file name of the target database.

Step 4.   Select an existing table name, or if selecting a table in another Access database, select **Another Database** and type a valid database drive, path, and file name in the **File Name** text box, and then select an existing table name. Choose **OK** when done.

Step 5.   Add the desired fields from table or query objects in the **Table Area**.

Step 6.   If there are differences in the field names between the append query and the destination table, use the **Append** cell in the **Field Grid** to indicate the destination field for each unmatched field in the query.

Step 7.   If you wish to limit the records added to the destination table, create criteria expressions in the appropriate field columns (in this case you may not use the *All Fields(*)* indicator - every field that participates in the append must be added manually to the **Field Grid**.

Step 8.   To view the records that will make up the new table, select the **View** button from the **Results** group or, to run the query, select the **Run** button from the

Results group.When you elect to *run* the query, a message box similar to the following will appear:

Step 9.   Choose **Yes** to append the rows or choose **No** to return to **Query Design View**. If you choose to append the row and errors are encountered, a message box similar to the following will appear:

Step 10.   If you encounter a message box similar to the one illustrated above, choose **Yes** to continue and ignore additional warnings or choose **No** to cancel the append query and return to **Query Design View**.

There is no undo command for appending records to another table.

If an error occurs during an append operation, the records that cause an error are not appended. Access does not create a table of the problematic records, but the error message presented when the query is run will attempt to group errors by type.

Update Query

An update query changes field values in an existing table based on specific criteria you provide. For example, if a department name changes, you would use an update query to search for all instances of the old department name (this would be the criteria the query uses) and replace those values with the new department name.

When you create an update query, a new row, **Update To**, is added to the **Field Grid**.

Points on Update Queries

- Update queries may only work against tables in the current database.

- Only add the field or fields that contain values to update or that will be used to supply criteria.

- You cannot update several fields independently in a single update query. Table fields matching any query field with a value in an **Update To** cell will be changed in any record where the query's criteria resolve to True. When in doubt, create multiple update queries, each designed to update values in a single field.

- You can use multiple fields to establish the criteria for an update and you can update multiple fields. Two or more table field values will be updated in any record where the criteria for the query resolves to True.

How to Create an Update Query

Step 1.　　From the **Create** ribbon, in the **Queries** group, choose **Query Design.**

Step 2.　　Using the **Show Tables** dialog box, add the table(s) and/or queries that will supply the field values. When finished, close the dialog by choosing **Close**.

Step 3.　　From the **Query Tools** ribbon in the **Query Type** group, select **Update Query**.

Step 4.　　Add the desired fields from the table object in the **Table Area**.

Step 5.　　For the field you wish to update, type a new field value in the **Update To** cell.

Step 6.　　Enter one or more criteria expressions in the appropriate **Criteria** cells. Keep in mind that only records where the query's criteria resolve to *True* will be updated. If you omit criteria every value in the target field will be updated.

Step 7.　　To view the records that will be updated, select the **View** button from the **Results** ribbon or, to run the query, from the **Results** ribbon, select **Run**. When you elect to run the query, a message box similar to the following will appear:

Step 8.　　Choose **Yes** to update the rows or choose **No** to return to **Query Design View**.

There is no undo command for updating records in a table.

Delete Query

Delete queries remove entire records from a table. If you need to remove specific records, you should specify one or more criteria to use when determining which records are deleted. When you create a delete query, a new row, **Delete**, appears in the **Field Grid**. The two options, **From** and **Where** are automatically selected by Access depending upon whether you are building a delete query to remove all records (From) or a subset of records (Where). The presence of a criteria expression controls this choice.

A delete query always deletes entire records, not specific field values. If you need to delete the data in one or more fields, consider creating an update query where the data in the target fields is updated to *empty* or *Null*.

Points on Delete Queries

- Generally you should add the All Fields indicator (*) to the **Field Grid**. This reinforces the idea that all field values from a target record will be deleted.

- If you only add a subset of the target table's fields and the criteria you establish are met, all field values for those records are deleted, not just the values in the fields displayed in the **Field Grid**.

- Delete queries run against tables joined to other tables where referential integrity has been established may result in a cascade delete operation. This is true for any target table that is joined to another table in a one-to-many join, where the target table is on the one side of the join.

- If related records will be deleted due to referential integrity constraints, the records from the related tables will not be displayed in the query's **Datasheet View** unless the related tables and their fields are included in the **Query Design View**.

- There is no undo command for a delete query. Once the query has been run the effect is permanent. It is strongly advised that you pay close attention to the records displayed in **Datasheet View**, to ensure that the query will work as expected. You may also wish to create a backup copy of the target table (or the entire database) before running the query.

How to Create a Delete Query

Step 1.   From the **Create** ribbon, in the **Queries** group, choose **Query Design.**

Step 2.   Using the **Show Tables** dialog box, add the table(s) and/or queries that will supply the field values. When finished, close the dialog by choosing **Close**.

Step 3.   From the **Query Tools** ribbon in the **Query Type** group, select **Delete Query**.

Step 4.   Add the *All Fields* indicator (*) from the table containing the record or records to delete.

Step 5.   If you wish to establish criteria, add the field or fields you will use to the **Field Grid**.

Step 6.   For any field that will serve to establish criteria, ensure that the **Delete** cell displays the option **Where**. Note that the only **Delete** cell that should display **From** is the *All Fields* column.

Step 7.   Enter one or more criteria expressions in the appropriate **Criteria** cells. Keep in mind that only records where the query's criteria resolve to *True* will be deleted.

Step 8.   To view the records that will be deleted, select the **View** button from the **Results** group, or, to run the query, from the **Results** group, select **Run**.

When you elect to run the query, a message box similar to the following will appear:

Step 9.   Choose **Yes** to delete the rows or choose **No** to return to **Query Design View**.

   If you do not establish any criteria in a delete query, it will delete *all* records from the target table.

   There is no undo command for deleting records from a table.

SQL Action Query Statements

Access implements the SQL standard for append, update, and delete queries. The Access version of the make table query maps to a variant of SQL understood by many but not all database management systems.

Care should be taken when creating SQL action queries, especially if you intend on running them from within a VBA procedure - Access will not issue warning dialog boxes when an action query is executed in this manner. The query will simply run. If you run an SQL action query from the **RunSQL** action in a macro, Access will warn you of the impending change in a manner similar to running an action query using the **Run** button from **Query Design View**.

SQL Statement	Description
SELECT tblProjects.* INTO tblArchiveProjects FROM tblProjects;	Creates a new table, *tblArchiveProjects* and copies all data from the *tblProjects* table into it.
SELECT tblProjects.* INTO tblArchiveProjects FROM tblProjects WHERE (((tblProjects.ProjectStartDate)<#1/1/2000#));	As above but only copies projects with a start date prior to the year 2000.
SELECT tblProjects.ProjectName, tblProjects.ProjectManager INTO tblArchiveProjects FROM tblProjects;	Creates a new table, *tblArchiveProjects* with only two fields from the *tblProjects* table: ProjectName and ProjectManager. All records from *tblProjects* are copied but only for those two fields.
INSERT INTO tblArchiveProjects (ID, ProjectName, ProjectManager, ProjectStartDate, ProjectEndDate, ProjectDescription) SELECT tblProjects.ID, tblProjects.ProjectName, tblProjects.ProjectManager, tblProjects.ProjectStartDate, tblProjects.ProjectEndDate, tblProjects.ProjectDescription FROM tblProjects WHERE (((tblProjects.ProjectStartDate)>#12/31/201 0#));	Appends the fields *ID, ProjectName, ProjectManager, ProjectStartDate, ProjectEndDate*, and *Description* into the existing table *tblArchiveProjects* but only for records in *tblProjects* where the ProjectStartDate is later than the year 2010. As mentioned in the section on Append Queries, if you employ a criteria you must manually add all the desired output fields. Using a criteria along with the *All Fields* * indicator will generate an error.
UPDATE tblStaffInfo SET tblStaffInfo.LastName = "Warren" WHERE (((tblStaffInfo.FirstName)="Amanda") AND ((tblStaffInfo.LastName)="Jones"));	Changes Amanda Jones to Amanda Warren in the tblStaffInfo table
UPDATE tblProjects SET Status = "Completed";	Changes every field value in the *Status* field of the *tblProjects* table to "Completed".
DELETE tblProjects.*, tblProjects.ProjectStartDate FROM tblProjects WHERE (((tblProjects.ProjectStartDate)<#1/1/2000#));	Deletes records in the *tblProjects* table where the *ProjectStartDate* is before the year 2000.
DELETE * FROM tblProjects;	Removes *all* records from the *tblProjects* table.

Chapter 11 | SQL Queries

The select and action queries discussed so far have all involved use of the **Query Design View**, a graphical design tool that has made query creation easy. For each query you create in **Query Design View** there is an underlying version of that query expressed in SQL (typically pronounced by speaking out each letter separately), or *Structured Query Language*. For any query you create you can view the SQL version by selecting **SQL** from the **View** or **Results** group.

There are three additional query types that are only related by the fact that they may not be designed using the **Query Design View**. These queries must be created in **SQL** view by entering valid SQL statements. These three query types are:

- **Union Query** - used to combine one or more fields from two or more tables.

- **Pass-Through Query** - connects directly to an ODBC-compliant database server. Open Database Connectivity (ODBC) is a standard that nearly all production database servers (such as Microsoft SQL Server, Oracle, and MySQL) adhere to.

- **Data Definition Query** - creates, modifies, and/or deletes tables, indices, and/or relational joins using SQL statements but only against the current database. If you need to conduct this type of operation against another database, use a pass-through query instead.

About SQL

SQL is the standard query language used by the majority of database systems - including Microsoft Access and all major databases such as Microsoft SQL Server, Oracle, and MySQL. As a computer language it is part of the ANSI (American National Standards Institute) and the ISO (International Standards Organization) standards. Although Microsoft Access only implements a subset of this rich language. For Select and Action queries, you can easily move between the **Query Design View** and **SQL View** to effectively toggle between the graphical query design we've experienced throughout this book and the underlying SQL version of the query.

Discussion of the specific syntax for SQL is beyond the scope of this book but the language is fairly straightforward and for the purpose of discussing union and pass-through queries we'll stay with examples that consist of simple select queries that pull data from a single table.

In essence, a SQL statement for a select query consists of two or three distinct sections:

- An initial SELECT clause followed by a list of output fields or an asterisk (*) which serves as the *all fields* indicator .

- A FROM clause followed by the name of the table containing the fields, and optionally

- A WHERE clause followed by one or more *criteria expressions*.

The following table cites 4 SQL examples of a simple Select query.

SQL Statement	Description
SELECT * FROM tblStaffInfo;	Returns all records from the tblStaffInfo table.
SELECT FirstName, LastName, Department FROM tblStaffInfo;	Returns three fields and all records from the tblStaffInfo table.
SELECT * FROM tblStaffInfo WHERE Department='IT';	Returns all fields from the tblStaffInfo table but only for those records where Department is IT.
SELECT FirstName, LastName FROM tblStaffInfo WHERE Department="IT";	Returns First and Last Name values from tblStaffInfo table but only for those records where Department is IT.

 One quick and easy way to familiarize yourself with SQL is to toggle between **Query Design View** and **SQL View** when creating a Select or Append query. In these cases the graphical design you're used to working with will be faithfully converted into valid SQL syntax.

Union Query

A union query merges one or more fields from two or more tables into a single result set. In essence, a union query combines the results of two or more separate select queries. The requirements for a union query are:

- Each select query must have the same number of result fields and they must be of the same data type or of a compatible data type. Generally this isn't an issue as Access will attempt to coerce data types in order to present results.

- If each select query has two or more result fields, the order of the output fields must be the same for each query participating in the union.

Union queries are useful in cases where you need to temporarily merge data from two or more tables. For example, if you maintain separate tables for volunteer and paid staff information, a union query would permit you to combine the names from the two separate tables. In the following example, first and last name, city, state, and postal code are combined from two tables. Note that an additional value, STATUS, is also added to indicate whether the merged data from the union query are derived from a volunteer or staff table.

The results of such a union query would appear similar to the following:

The observant reader may have noticed that the fifth output field was named differently between the two tables. In the Volunteer table it is named *PostalCode* while in the Staff table the field is named *ZipCode*. In these instances, Access uses the first-named example for the result set.

In the example above, note that a "new" field, *Status* was created in both select statements. The terms *"volunteer"* and *"staff"* in the field list inform SQL to use the quote-delimited values in the results, making it easy to determine staff from volunteers.

How to Create a Union Query

Since SQL-specific queries may not involve the **Query Design View** this procedure bypasses the selection of tables.

Step 1.   From the **Create** ribbon, in the **Queries** group, choose **Query Design.**

Step 2.   From **Show Tables** dialog box, choose **Close**.

 If you do select a table from the **Show Tables** dialog and continue with this procedure, the SQL statement SELECT FROM *tablename* will appear in the SQL editor.

Step 3.   From the **Query Tools** ribbon in the **Query Type** group, select **Union Query**. The **Query Design View** will change to the **SQL Editor**.

Step 4.   Enter a valid Select SQL statement to pull records from the first table. You may switch to **DataSheet View** to verify that your query works as expected. Return to **SQL View** to continue.

Step 5.   Press *Enter* and type the term UNION. Press *Enter* again.

Step 6.   Enter a valid SELECT SQL statement to pull records from the second table.

Step 7.   If you intend to pull records from three or more tables, repeat steps 5 and 6.

Step 8.   To view the results of your union query, change to **Datasheet** View.

Step 9.   If desired, save your query by choosing **Save** from the **Quick Access Toolbar**.

Pass-Through Query

This type of query creates an interaction between Microsoft Access and an ODBC-compliant database. The latter is typically a database server such as Microsoft SQL Server, Oracle, MySQL, or a host of other applications. Using a pass-through query, you can work with data stored on a server from within the Access environment. There are several points to consider when using pass-through queries:

- Unfortunately, between Microsoft Access and the database servers there isn't full compliance with either the ANSI or ISO standard for the SQL language. When creating SQL statements for a pass-through query you will need to write the statement in the variant of SQL that the distant database server understands. If you intend to connect to data on a Microsoft SQL Server you'll need to write your SQL statements to be understood by SQL Server. Likewise when attempting to connect to a MySQL or an Oracle database server.

- Database servers are sophisticated applications that generally employ advanced security. Prior to creating a pass-through query you may have to interact with the administrator of the target database for sufficient permissions. You'll also need to know the valid names of any tables and their fields in order to successfully connect.

- ODBC connections are mediated through objects called DSN (Data Source Name), which are managed by the Windows operating system. We'll briefly outline how to create a DSN as this object should be created and tested prior to creating a pass-through query.

How to Create a DSN for a Pass-Through Query

The specific details to open the **ODBC Data Source Administrator** vary between versions of the Windows operating system. For earlier versions you generally go to the control panel and choose **Administrative Tools**, then select ODBC. In later versions the quick approach is to type **ODBC** in the **Search programs and files** box located at the bottom of the **Start** menu. This procedure assumes that the **ODBC Data Source Administrator** is open. It should appear similar to the following:

Step 1.   From the **ODBC Data Source Administrator**, choose the **System DSN** tab, then select **Add**.

Step 2.   From the list of available drivers, choose the driver appropriate to the target data source. For example, if intending to connect to a Microsoft SQL Server database you would choose *SQL Server*. Choose **Finish**.

 If the desired driver isn't listed you may need to install it first. Vendors of the major database servers all offer drivers required to connect to their product via an ODBC connection.

Step 3.   In the **Create a New Data** Source dialog box, provide a descriptive name for the DSN you are creating, a brief description of the DSN (optional) and select the server you wish to connect to. In some computing environments one or more servers may appear in the **Server** drop down box. In other environments you may need to manually enter a server name or a URL (example: \\192.168.1.177 *or* \\DATASTORE). Select **Next** when ready.

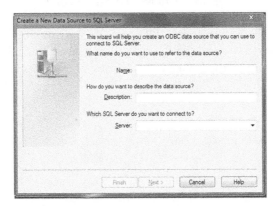

Step 4.   The remaining steps will be dependent upon the specific server application you are working with. Essentially you'll need to specify a valid username and password (these will be determined by the database administrator of the server you wish to connect to), as well as the name of the target database (servers frequently maintain tens to hundreds of individual databases). The process will end with a dialog box similar to the following:

Step 5.   Choose the **Test Data Source** button to confirm that your settings are correct and that you can connect to the target database. If you encounter difficulties, you may need to consult with the database administrator of the target server for assistance. If you are successful, choose **OK** to complete the DSN creation.

How to Create a Pass-Through Query

This procedure assumes that you have a working DSN for the target database server and that you have sufficient permissions on that server to select data from a table.

Step 1.   From the **Create** ribbon, in the **Queries** group, choose **Query Design.**

Step 2.   From **Show Tables** dialog box, choose **Close.**

 If you do select a table from the **Show Tables** dialog and continue with this procedure, the SQL statement SELECT FROM *tablename* will appear in the SQL editor.

Step 3.   From the **Query Tools** ribbon in the **Query Type** group, select **Pass-Through Query**. The **Query Design View** will change to the SQL Editor.

Step 4.   From the **Show/Hide** group, choose **Property Sheet**. The Property Sheet dialog box will appear similar to the following.

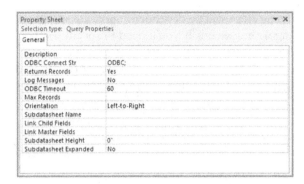

Step 5.   Click in the **OBDC Connect Str** text area, then select the **Builder** (...) button.

Step 6.   From the **Select Data Source** dialog box, choose the **Machine Data Source** tab, then select the desired DSN.

Step 7.   Depending upon the server you are connecting to, you may be prompted for a username and/or password. Enter the requested information to continue.

Step 8.   If you were prompted to enter a password, Access will ask if you want to store the password in the connection string. It is recommended that you choose **No** as otherwise the password will appear as plain text in the **ODBC Connect Str** text area.

Step 9.   Once the **ODBC Connect Str** text area has the DSN information you are ready to create your SQL statement. Close the **Property Sheet** to return to the **SQL View**. Enter a valid SQL statement. Remember to create the statement using the variant of SQL that the target server understands.

Step 10.   To run your query choose **Datasheet View** from the **Results** group.

Some pass-through queries may request a record set that contains hundreds of thousands of records. You may wish to run versions of your pass-through queries on the actual database server first to ensure you are receiving the desired query results and then migrate the query to Microsoft Access.

You may also adjust the **Max Records** property of the query to limit the number of records returned.

Data Definition Query

A part of the SQL language specification are statements, collectively referred to as *Data Definition Language*, which create, modify, or delete tables, fields, and/or indices. Microsoft Access recognizes a subset of the Data Definition Language. You can create data definition queries that will create or delete tables, create or delete fields within a table, create or delete a table index, or a relationship join between tables.

The main reason one might wish to create data definition queries is to automate some process. Although the topic is beyond the scope of this book, it is possible to automate Microsoft Access using the Visual Basic for Applications (VBA) programming language. Using VBA and queries written in Data Definition Language you could elicit actions such as creating a temporary table to store data, report on that data, and then delete the temporary table.

The following table lists a few examples of data definition queries.

SQL Statement	Description
CREATE TABLE tblTemp (ID COUNTER NOT NULL UNIQUE CONSTRAINT ID PRIMARY KEY, FirstName CHAR(15), LastName CHAR(20));	Creates a table, *tblTemp*, with three fields. *ID* (a numeric autonumber field that is the Primary Key, *FirstName* - text storing 15 characters, and *LastName* - text storing 20 characters.
DROP TABLE tblTemp	Deletes the table *tblTemp* from the database.
ALTER TABLE tblTemp DROP COLUMN LastName;	Deletes the column *LastName* from table *tblTemp*
ALTER TABLE tblTemp ADD COLUMN Surname CHAR(25);	Adds a column, *Surname* - text 25 characters - to the table *tblTemp*.
ALTER TABLE tblStaffSkills ADD CONSTRAINT fkStaffSkills FOREIGN KEY (StaffID) REFERENCES tblStaffInfo (ID);	Adds a one-to-many join between *tblStaffInfo* (1 side of join) and *tblStaffSkills* (many side of join). The join is named *fkStaffSkills*.

If you use a data definition query to create a new table, to add a new column to an existing table, or to change the data type of an existing column, use one of the following supported *Data Types* to specify what kind of data the column will store. Note that some data types, available to you via the **Table Design Editor** are not available through the data definition language. These are *Autonumber ReplicationID, Hyperlink,* and *Lookup Field.*

Data Type	Comment
BYTE	Whole number within the range 0 to 255.
COUNTER	Creates an *autonumber* field.
CURRENCY	Creates a *currency* data type with 1 to 4 decimal places.
DATETIME, DATE	Both terms are synonyms for a Date/Time field.
DOUBLE, NUMBER	Synonyms for a real number field of the *double* field size - this creates an 8-bit number that can manage up to 13 decimal points.
GUID	A replication ID (in Access, a number of the *ReplicationID* field size).
INTEGER	A whole number in the range +/- 2 billion.
LONG BINARY	A whole number falling in the range +/-2,147,483,647.
MEMO	A text field capable of storing up to 63,999 characters.
SINGLE	A number field storing a real number with up to 4 decimal points.
SMALLINT	A whole number within the range +/- 32,000.
TEXT(*n*), CHAR(*n*), VARCHAR(*n*)	A text field containing 1-255 characters, specified by *n*.
YESNO	A Boolean field storing true/false, or yes/no values.

In addition to the above data types, any field you specify may also contain the following clauses.

Clause	Comment
NOT NULL	Indicates that the field may not store null or empty values.
UNIQUE	Creates a unique index on the field. Duplicate values are not allowed.
CONSTRAINT *name* PRIMARY KEY	Creates a single-field primary key. In the index for the table the primary key index will be given the value specified by *name*.

Once a table has been created, you may also create one or more indices on one or more fields within the table. The following examples illustrate index creation.

SQL Statement	Description
CREATE INDEX myIndex ON tblTemp (LastName ASC);	Creates an index named *myIndex* that orders the values in the field *LastName* in the *tblTemp* table in ascending order.
CREATE UNIQUE INDEX myIndex ON tblTemp (LastName ASC, FirstName DESC);	Establishes a unique index (no duplicates in the LastName and FirstName fields) in the table *tblTemp*. The index orders last names in alphabetical order and first names in reverse alphabetical order. Thus in the index, Zebulon Smith would appear before Abe Smith.
CREATE UNIQUE INDEX myIndex ON tblTemp (LastName ASC, FirstName DESC) WITH DISALLOW NULL;	As the previous example except no FirstName or LastName fields may be null or empty.
DROP INDEX myIndex ON tblTemp;	Removes the index *myIndex* from the *tblTemp* table.

How to Create a Data Definition Query

This type of query may only act on the current database. If you need to create or modify objects in another database, use a pass-through query instead (and remember that you would use the distant server's dialect of SQL - not Access' version).

Step 1.   From the **Create** ribbon, in the **Queries** group, choose **Query Design.**

Step 2.   From **Show Tables** dialog box, choose **Close**.

 If you do select a table from the **Show Tables** dialog and continue with this procedure, the SQL statement SELECT FROM *tablename* will appear in the SQL editor.

Step 3.   From the **Query Tools** ribbon in the **Query Type** group, select **Data Definition Query**. The **Query Design View** will change to the SQL Editor.

Step 4.   Type a valid SQL statement. If desired, use the tables in this section as a guide.

Step 5.   To run your data definition query, choose **Run** from the **Results** group.

 Access will not prompt you with a warning when a data definition query deletes an index, column, or a table from the database. Deleting a table from the database is not a reversible action.

Appendix A | Staff and Projects Database

The samples in this manual illustrate a simple staff and projects database – a design that might commonly be used in an organization that tracks information about staff (contact methods and skills) as well as information about projects (here the main interest is in the staffing of projects as well as the budget for a project). A copy of this database may be downloaded from www.sycamoretechnicalpress.com

The basic relationships between the tables used in the sample database appear in the following illustration.

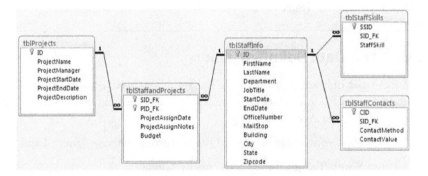

The structure of the 5 tables, and if applicable, the indices used to maintain uniqueness among rows, are presented below.

tblStaffInfo

This table, along with tblProjects, can be considered the two main tables in the staff and projects database. A primary key affords an easy way to relate a staff record to other tables and an index based on staff first and last name as well as department enforce uniqueness for each row.

Field Name	Data Type	Description
ID	AutoNumber	Primary Key
FirstName	Text	
LastName	Text	
Department	Text	
JobTitle	Text	
StartDate	Date/Time	
EndDate	Date/Time	
OfficeNumber	Text	
MailStop	Text	
Building	Text	
City	Text	

There are two indices for tblStaffInfo. The primary key is automatically created by Access. The index **Staff** asserts that no two records may contain the same staff first and last name and department.

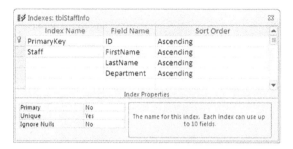

tblProjects

Along with tblStaffInfo this table constitutes the other major table in the Staff and Projects database. Both tables store information about the two realms the database focuses on. Like the tblStaffInfo table, a second index **Project** enforces uniqueness by assuming the combination of project name, project manager, and start date will not be repeated.

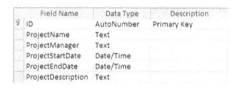

The indexes for tblProjects appears as:

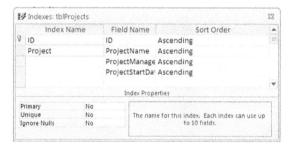

tblStaffContact

This table relates the one-to-many ways you can contact each staff member. An index based on the foreign key for the staff ID, the contact method, and the contact value, ensure that no two rows are duplicated.

Field Name	Data Type	Description
CID	AutoNumber	Primary Key
SID_FK	Number	Foreign key to tblStaffInfo Primary Key
ContactMethod	Text	
ContactValue	Text	

The index appears as follows:

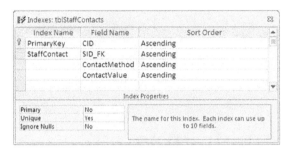

Index Name	Field Name	Sort Order
PrimaryKey	CID	Ascending
StaffContact	SID_FK	Ascending
	ContactMethod	Ascending
	ContactValue	Ascending

Index Properties

Primary	No	
Unique	Yes	The name for this index. Each index can use up to 10 fields.
Ignore Nulls	No	

tblStaffSkills

Similar to tblStaffContacts, this table stores any skills associated with each staff member.

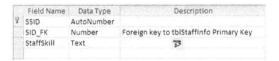

Field Name	Data Type	Description
SSID	AutoNumber	
SID_FK	Number	Foreign key to tblStaffInfo Primary Key
StaffSkill	Text	

The index, based on the staff foreign key and staff skill, ensures uniqueness for each row:

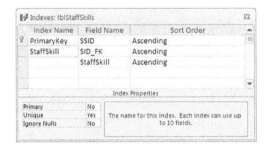

Index Name	Field Name	Sort Order
PrimaryKey	SSID	Ascending
StaffSkill	SID_FK	Ascending
	StaffSkill	Ascending

Index Properties

Primary	No	
Unique	Yes	The name for this index. Each index can use up to 10 fields.
Ignore Nulls	No	

tblStaffandProjects

The final table is the only bridge table in this design. Its purpose is to manage the information that relates to project staffing. Each project may have one or more staff assigned to it, and ultimately, each staff member may be assigned to zero or more projects. It is also the only table in the database design to utilize two fields which together make up the table's primary key: the foreign key to the tblStaffInfo primary key and the foreign key to the tblProjects primary key. Using these two fields together ensures uniqueness among the rows and enforces the logical requirement that no staff can be assigned to a project more than once. This simple design removes any requirement for an additional index to enforce uniqueness among the records.

Further, in this design the budget field implies that each staff member is given an individual budget for their part in a project. Recall from the discussion on banded reports that even given this configuration, with a project staffed by several members from the same department, one can easily generate a report that groups project staffing information by department, with the purpose of providing totals of the budget amount both by staff, by department, and by project.

Field Name	Data Type	Description
SID_FK	Number	Foreign key to tblStaffInfo primary key
PID_FK	Number	Foreign key to tblProjects primary key
ProjectAssignDate	Date/Time	
ProjectAssignNotes	Memo	
Budget	Currency	

Index

About the Author

F. Mark Schiavone was originally trained as a research scientist, and in that capacity he began constructing database applications and analyzing complex data sets over 30 years ago. His database skills include Microsoft Access, Microsoft SQL Server and MySQL and he has constructed applications using those platforms for clients in large to mid-size organizations, including the US Department of Education, the National Weather Service, and the International Monetary Fund. He has authored over 30 training titles in topics such as Microsoft Access, Microsoft Word, Microsoft Excel, and in the VBA programming language. Each title was designed with the busy office technology worker in mind and focuses on important and useful tasks.

Along with his partner John he has restored three stone houses (two of which were 18th century while the most recent house dates from 1835), reroofed a loafing barn, disassembled and reassembled a corn crib, and built several frame houses, additions or outbuildings. He has designed every new structure built on their property. He is a passionate all weather, high mileage motorcyclist and is usually the only motorcyclist on the local roads when the temperature is below 25° F.

Cover design by Martha A. Loomis.

www.ingramcontent.com/pod-product-compliance
Lightning Source LLC
Chambersburg PA
CBHW080422060326
40689CB00019B/4345